I0801970

HIDDEN HISTORY *of* CUMBERLAND COUNTY

HIDDEN HISTORY *of* CUMBERLAND COUNTY

Joseph David Cress

THE History PRESS

Published by The History Press
Charleston, SC 29403
www.historypress.net

Copyright © 2013 by Joseph David Cress
All rights reserved

First published 2013

Manufactured in the United States

ISBN 978.1.60949.990.7

Library of Congress CIP data applied for.

Notice: The information in this book is true and complete to the best of our knowledge. It is offered without guarantee on the part of the author or The History Press. The author and The History Press disclaim all liability in connection with the use of this book.

All rights reserved. No part of this book may be reproduced or transmitted in any form whatsoever without prior written permission from the publisher except in the case of brief quotations embodied in critical articles and reviews.

Contents

Acknowledgements

As always, I thank my wife, Stacey, for her love, support and understanding through the many months of research and writing that goes into a manuscript.

Ten years ago, I married my best friend, and these have been the happiest years of my life. From you, my love, I've learned to be steadfast and focused in the midst of adversity. You are, without a doubt, the bravest person I've ever met. You are an inspiration.

My gratitude also goes out to all my friends and family who have encouraged me over the years and to past and present editors who challenged me to hone my skills. In this, I am especially thankful to have been part of the hardworking and dedicated staff of the *Sentinel* newspaper in Carlisle. Every day you strive to put out a quality product, and my many years spent at that cluttered desk have prepared me for the goal of being an author.

Lastly, I want to thank the professional and helpful staff of the Cumberland County Historical Society—in particular, photo archivist Richard Tritt and his crew for their work in helping me select and process the vast majority of the images found in this book.

Introduction

Welcome to the unknown, the overlooked and underrated. This book is for you, the visitor or local resident looking to brave the obscure pathways of Cumberland County history. Brace yourself going forward, for the journey ahead is beset with the schemes of a lady pirate, the nefarious work of kidnappers, bloodthirsty partisan politics and the nasty mudslinging of rival journalists. Take heart in knowing you will meet along the way such characters as the "Father of Penn State," a hero who disobeyed orders, a tinkerer hung up by a lack of funds and a "tramp" who helped to make the Smithsonian Institution into "America's attic." By the end, you will know of people, places and circumstances so fundamental in their influence that we have simply taken them for granted.

Cumberland County shares its name with a valley that arcs from the Susquehanna River in the east to the Potomac River in the southwest. From the beginning, this gateway to the western interior has served as a strategic transportation hub with strong ties to the military. It was through the Cumberland Valley in June 1863 that the Confederate Army of Northern Virginia came within miles of Harrisburg, the capital of Pennsylvania. As with any community, there are stories behind the scenes that shaped Cumberland County history but linger only on the fringes of our collective recall and understanding. I have chosen seventeen of those stories covering over two hundred years from the settlement of Shippensburg in 1733 to the end of rail service in downtown Carlisle in 1936. In between, you will read of moments of innovation and reform,

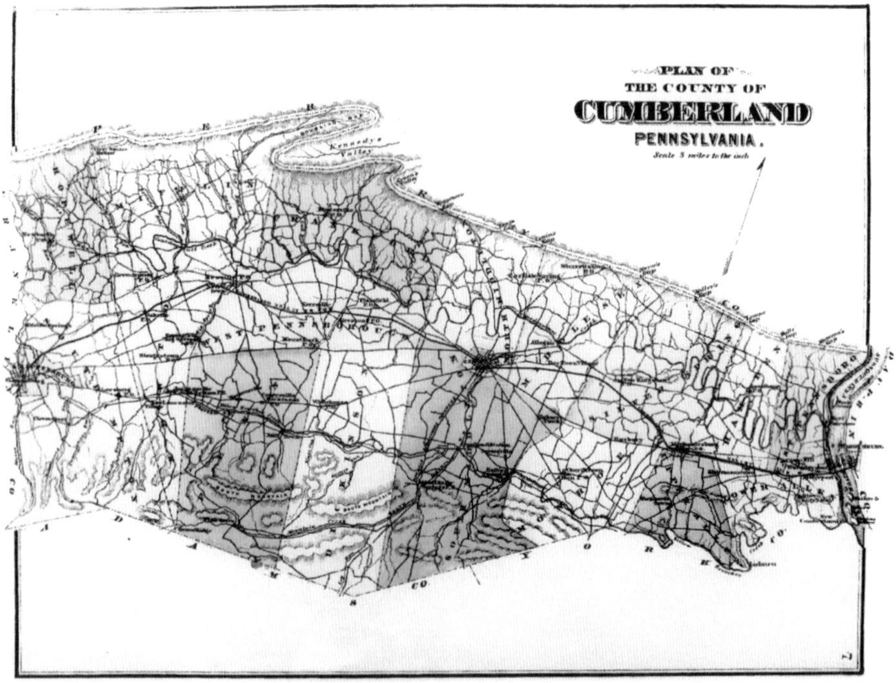

This map of Cumberland County was published in the 1872 Atlas by F.W. Beers & Co. *Courtesy of CCHS.*

defiance and desperation, legal wrangling and political intrigue played out across the whole of the county.

This book offers a mixed bag of history. There is true crime in the murder of a drifter and the revenge killing by his friend. There are court cases over the rights of fugitive slaves and the true inventor of the telephone. The Civil War is well represented with detailed accounts on the "Battle of Papertown," Medal of Honor recipient William Miller and the northernmost reach of the Confederate army during the Gettysburg campaign. There is turmoil in government over the necessity of the Bill of Rights and accusations of rigged elections that trigger the unknown and largely forgotten Buckshot War. There are stories on how the county led the way in the development of the first state police academy, the first Christmas savings club and the first sleeper car. Not to be outdone are tales of the military supply depot that helped to win the American Revolution and a field dressing crucial to saving countless lives during World War II.

As much as possible, I have used primary sources to tell each story from the participant point of view. I've found this approach to be far more engaging as it puts the reader in the midst of the action. History was never meant to be drab or dusty but active and alive in how it shapes society and its people. It is my hope you will find within these pages a doorway to open, a window to look through and a pathway to a better and broader understanding.

1733: Bloody Deed

They found what remained of Robert McInnis on the morning of the third day. He was sitting atop a slight knoll in the woods about a half-mile southeast of the village. His back was against a tree. His head was bowed on his breast. His clothing was soaked through with blood. Death had been by a bullet to the brain, fired from ambush by an unknown assailant. A gun owned by McInnis was found nearby, propped up against a tree, fully loaded. In one hand, the traveler held a letter written in a language strange to the Scotch-Irish settlers of the Cumberland Valley. The murder was a mystery so deeply unsettling suspicion soon turned to the Indians camped nearby. The villagers began to question the honesty of the natives and their offer of friendship.

Two days and nights had passed since McInnis went out to hunt game that summer of 1733. He told the villagers he would be back within a few hours but never returned. On the third day, Mrs. Dunlap recalled hearing a single gunshot echo through the wilderness from the southeast around noon the day McInnis disappeared. She told the other villagers, prompting them to organize a search party that set out in that direction. They found his decaying corpse seated on the ground. It was easy to lay the blame on the savages. None of the settlers were away from their homes on the day McInnis was killed. Who else could have committed the murder?

In his book *History of Cumberland County*, Reverend Conway Wing described the victim as a drifter "much esteemed for his talents and genial disposition." A native of Northern Ireland, McInnis had a commanding presence and powerful build. College educated, he studied law and was admitted to the bar just before he enlisted as an officer in the British army. He served for about a year before he resigned or sold his commission. McInnis then went to Spain, where he met and married a native woman around the time when he enlisted in the Spanish army. She was lost at sea off the French coast on her way to Ireland to join McInnis after he left the military. The letter McInnis was reading at the time of his murder was written by his wife in her native tongue.

It is said that McInnis had arrived in America on some business with the Penn family. He soon became acquainted with an Irish woman and followed her to the village that later became Shippensburg—the oldest town in the Cumberland Valley and, with the exception of York, the oldest in Pennsylvania west of the Susquehanna River. McInnis befriended an Indian who lived in a cabin near present-day Dykeman's Spring. A man of immense size, his nickname was Big Will, and he was as gentle as a child. Before the murder, the Indian mingled freely with the white settlers. After the crime, Big Will stayed away from them.

"This led some to suspect that he [Big Will] had committed the bloody deed," Wing wrote. "But it was well known…he never owned a gun and had never been known to use one. All his hunting was done with bow and arrow…When met by anyone after the death…and interrogated to his knowledge…he would talk mysteriously and shake his head and say, 'Big Will, no shoot gun.'" Before his death from an unspecified illness, this Giant of the Spring promised some white friends that in a few days he would reveal the identity of the Indian responsible for the murder of McInnis. He assured them the perpetrator was dead. "An arrow drank his blood, and wolves ate his flesh," Big Will had told them. He died before he could divulge the name.

"It was thought by many settlers the friendly attention that McInnis had put to this child of the forest had excited the envy of some red men of his tribe who killed him [McInnis] in order to deprive Will of these attentions," Wing wrote. It was believed that Big Will, upon learning the identity of the killer, took matters into his own hands and shot the man with an arrow to avenge the murder of his friend. The settlers buried McInnis on a hill north of the village. As for the gentle giant, his final resting place is a mystery. More than a century later, workers building the Cumberland Valley Railroad unearthed a skeleton of colossal proportions on the south end of Shippensburg. Who knows—maybe it was Big Will.

The murder of McInnis reinforced the fear that already existed among the settlers of an impending Indian attack. "There's a good ween of ingens around here," James Magraw wrote his brother John in a May 1733 letter. "I fear they intend to give us a great deal of trouble and may do us a great deal of harm." James had asked that word be sent to the governor of the Pennsylvania colony to have muskets shipped to the village. In the letter, James described the trip west from the Susquehanna River, the family cabin in the wilderness, the death and burial of a local girl and other aspects of village life. The following is an edited version with the misspellings removed:

> *We was three days on our journey coming from Harris Ferry here. We could not take much speed on account of the children. They could not get on as fast as Jane and me.*
>
> *I put it* [the cabin] *on a level piece of ground near the road or path in the woods at the foot of a hill. There is a fine stream of water that comes from a spring a half-a-mile south of where our cabin is built. I would have put it near the water, but the land is low and wet.*
>
> *Hugh Rippey's daughter Mary was buried yesterday, this will be sad news for Andrew Simpson...He is to come over in the fall when they were to be married. Mary was a very pretty girl; she died of a fever, and they buried her up on rising ground, north of the road or path where we made choice of a piece of ground for a graveyard. She was the first buried there. Poor Hugh has none left now but his wife, Sam, and little Isabel.*
>
> *There is plenty of timber south of us. We have eighteen cabins built here now, and it looks like a town, but we have no name for it.*
>
> *Come up soon, our cabin will be ready to go into in a week and you can go in till you get one built; we have planted some corn and potatoes.*

There is no record of white settlers in the Cumberland Valley prior to 1729. This region was mostly occupied by scattered tribes of Susquehannock and Shawnee Indians. The first Europeans to explore the valley were traders like James LeTort, who established a trading post where several native paths intersected near present-day Carlisle. In June 1730, twelve families crossed the river at Harris Ferry and followed an Indian path west through LeTort Spring and beyond to what is now the Shippensburg area. The path roughly followed the same course as present-day Route 11.

The majority of these settlers were Scotch-Irish. Reverend D. Homer Kendall wrote a book on the history of the Messiah Evangelical United Brethren Church in Shippensburg. In it, Kendall described the Scotch-Irish as a "hardy, brave, hotheaded group of people excitable in temper and unrestrainable in passion—their hand open to a friend as it was clenched

Pennsylvania ss.
George the Sec
George Stevenson of the Coun
Confidence in your
Counties of York and Cumber
better known,
made Capital, or Felonies of
and Cumberland aforesaid,
whom and to whom,
concerning the Premises
other the Premises according
Sentence to pronounce and
Giving hereby and Granting
appoint some honest and
in the Premises who shall
You the said Edward Shippen
to deliver the Gaols of the Co
being for any Crime or Crime
at certain Days which You,
the said Counties of York and
the Premises, and hear and dete
in Form aforesaid, Acting alwa
Amerciaments and other Thing
Counties of York and Cumber
cause to come there before You,
and such honest and lawful
Matters concerning the Prem
caused the Great Seal of Our sa
Morris Esquire (by Vertu
Esquires true and absolute Pr
Governor and Commander
upon Delaware at Philade
Thousand Seven Hundred a

the Grace of God of Great Britain France and Ireland
To Edward Shippen Sen.r of the County of Lancaster,
and John Armstrong of the County of Cumberland in Our
Greeting Know Ye that reposing Special Trust and
Prudence and Ability We have assigned You, or any Two of
or Solemn Affirmations of honest and lawful Men of the said
every of them, by whom the Truth of the Matter may be the
, or such other Crimes as are by the Laws of Our said Province
and the Accessaries thereunto, within the Counties of York
soever or howsoever had, done, perpetrated, or committed, and by
what manner, and of other Matters and Circumstances in anywise
them; and to hear and determine the said Treasons, Murders and
and upon Conviction of any Person or Persons, Judgment or
Execution thereupon to award as the Law doth or shall direct
the said Justices, or any Two of You, full Power and Authority to
son to be by You duly qualified to be Clerk of your Proceedings
record the same for Preservation And We have also appointed
and John Armstrong or any Two of You Our Justices
York and Cumberland aforesaid of the Prisoners in the same
, or Felonies aforesaid, And therefore We command You that
of You, shall consider of, You meet together at the Court Houses of
nd, to deliver the said Gaols, and make diligent Enquiry of and upon
and singular the same Premises, and do and accomplish those Things
as to Justice according to Law shall appertain Saving to Us the
reof belonging For We have commanded the Sheriffs of the said
at certain Days which You shall make known to them to
risoners of the said Gaols and their Attachments, as also so many
several Bailywicks as may be necessary by whom the Truth of
be the better known and enquired In Testimony whereof We have
ce to be hereunto affixed Witness Robert Hunter
mission from Thomas Penn and Richard Penn
of the said Province) with Our Royal Approbation Lieutenant
Province aforesaid and Counties of Newcastle Kent and Sussex
Ninth Day of October in the Year of our Lord One
Five and in the Twenty Ninth Year of Our Reign

This document dated October 9, 1755, appointed Edward Shippen III one of three justices for York and Cumberland Counties. *Courtesy of CCHS.*

against an enemy." This group first entered the Cumberland Valley in large numbers in September 1736 after one thousand families had journeyed from Belfest, Ireland, to Pennsylvania.

While the Scotch-Irish would gradually move west in pursuit of fresh adventure on the frontier, they were closely followed by the Germans "who were good judges of land, worked hard and practiced economy with plodding industry and steadfastness," Kendall wrote. He explained how it was Germans who permanently occupied the land after the Scotch-Irish had moved through. This settlement pattern caused such a demand for land that it prompted a major purchase in 1736 of Indian territory. William Penn wanted to negotiate in good faith with the native tribes while preventing Maryland from laying claim to lands west of the Susquehanna River. He authorized Samuel Blunston to act as an agent in the negotiations for the purchase and to grant licenses for settlers already moving into the Cumberland Valley.

A deal was struck with the Indians, and the valley was purchased from them on October 25, 1736. A land office was opened the following January. Among the items paid to the Indians for the valley were six hundred pounds of lead, five hundred pounds of gunpowder, forty-five guns, one hundred blankets, forty hats, forty pairs of shoes, forty pairs of stockings, one hundred hatchets, five hundred knives, 120 combs, two thousand needles, twenty-four looking glasses, two pounds of vermillion, twenty-five gallons of rum, two hundred pounds of tobacco and one thousand pipes. Two years prior to the opening of the land office, Cumberland Valley settlers petitioned the courts to lay out a Great Road from Harris Ferry to the Potomac River. When the course of the road was finally plotted in 1744, Shippensburg was the only village on the route.

To protect the land claims of Pennsylvania, William Penn wanted to establish a settlement as far down the valley and as close to the Maryland border as possible. In early 1737, he granted his longtime friend Edward Shippen III of Lancaster land patents totaling 1,312 acres that included the area first settled by the twelve families back in June 1730. A wealthy merchant, Shippen laid out the town that now bears his name around 1749, but leases were not issued to settlers until 1763. During the War for Independence, Shippen furnished supplies to the Continental army. His son, Edward Shippen IV, became the father-in-law of an infamous traitor when his daughter Margaret Shippen became the second wife of Benedict Arnold.

It is believed the first settlers of what became Shippensburg set up a temporary camp among the rocks along Burd's Run on the east end of town. They then moved to higher ground on the Indian trail. The first cabins were built near what is today Queen Street. The trail became the main street, which was named King. Where the two streets crossed became the town center at which was placed the town pump, a whipping post and a store operated by Francis Campble, the first merchant to open for business in the settlement. Campble came over to Philadelphia from Northern Ireland in 1733 and soon became friends with Edward Shippen III, who gave glowing reviews of land west of the Susquehanna River. In the fall of 1737, Campble left Philadelphia with Shippen to visit the settlement. The vast majority of these first settlers were Presbyterian, and nearly all their churches were built near a spring or a stream. Located two miles northeast of Shippensburg, Middle Spring Church dates from 1738 and is perhaps the oldest place of worship in Cumberland County.

Growing unease toward local Indians prompted the settlers to convene a meeting in the spring of 1740 at the stone house that still stands at the southwest corner of East King and South Queen Streets. Built in 1735 as a private residence, this building became a tavern operated by a widow named Janet Piper. At the meeting, the villagers decided to build a log fort on the northeast side of their settlement to serve as a refuge in the event of an Indian attack. A time was scheduled for the people to assemble and cut logs, and the fort was completed in a few days. In the fall of 1740, Deputy Governor George Thomas dispatched a garrison of twenty-two men to the fort. At the time, the log structure had no name. It became Fort Franklin in 1755 to distinguish it from Fort Morris, which was then under construction on a rocky hill on the west end of town.

The Piper Tavern played another role as the first courthouse of the newly formed Cumberland County. In 1749, valley residents presented a petition before the provincial assembly asking that land west of the Susquehanna River and north and west of York County be erected into a county called Cumberland. At the time, the valley was under the jurisdiction of Lancaster County. The residents felt the remoteness of the valley to the county seat made it easier for criminals to evade justice. Their petition was granted on January 27, 1750, and Shippensburg, being the only substantial settlement in the valley, was designated temporary county seat. Since the tavern already served as a popular venue for public meetings, it became the site of the first court of justice in Cumberland County on July 24, 1750. In the first case heard, Bridget Hagen was convicted of stealing money from Jacob Long and was sentenced to fifteen lashes on her bare back at the public whipping post. She also had to pay six pounds, seven shillings and six pence in restitution.

Three more court terms were held at the tavern with the last taking place on April 24, 1751. In the interim, the governor had appointed deputy surveyor

This circa 1906 postcard by C.L. Laughlin shows Piper Tavern, the first Cumberland County courthouse. *Courtesy of CCHS.*

Thomas Cookson of Lancaster to evaluate the merits of four proposed locations for a permanent county seat, including Shippensburg. In the end, Cookson recommended that the county seat be moved to the area around the LeTort Spring Run, where Indian trader James LeTort had first established a trading post roughly two decades before. This suggestion was approved, a courthouse and jail were built and the town that became Carlisle was laid out.

The change in status upset many prominent Shippensburg area residents, who wrote letters in protest claiming the location of Carlisle as county seat would be inconvenient for many citizens living in the more remote parts of Cumberland County. When Carlisle was founded in 1751, the county was much larger, extending from the Susquehanna River west to present-day Pittsburgh. The decision generated so much bile that some claimed that Cookson had been bribed to misrepresent the facts that favored retaining Shippensburg as the county seat. David Magaw accused Cookson of lying on his report to the governor when the surveyor said one of his chief objections to keeping the court in Shippensburg was scarcity of water.

The fact is, there were supporters for each of the four locations reviewed by Cookson. The surveyor recommended Carlisle because it was located near plentiful sources of water, pasture, timber, stone and other materials necessary to support a town. The LeTort Spring Run location was at the crossroads of existing paths that supported trade with both the Indian tribes and the city of Philadelphia. It had quality soil and was close to both the Yellow Breeches and Conodoguinet Creeks. Even then, Carlisle only had five dwellings as late as May 1753 compared to Shippensburg, which was a much larger community. As for the tavern, it deteriorated over time and was put up for sale in 1926. Four local men came forward to purchase the historic structure and turn it over to the Shippensburg Civic Club, whose members raised the money to restore the building to its original condition.

Population growth slowed down after 1751. Historians believe this drop in activity was not caused by the removal of the county seat to Carlisle. Instead, the Shippensburg area was subjected to off-and-on Indian attacks from 1753 to 1764 that caused widespread alarm. For part of that period, Pennsylvania was in the midst of the French and Indian War—the name given to the North American front of a broader global conflict between France and Great Britain. In the spring of 1755, laborers were building a road west out of Shippensburg in preparation for a summer campaign against Fort Duquesne,

This watercolor by Frank R. Bagley depicts Carlisle as it may have looked in 1753, two years after it became the county seat. The image is based on a letter written by John O'Neal, a surveyor. *Courtesy of CCHS.*

a key French base guarding the strategic forks at present-day Pittsburgh where the Alleghany and Monongahela Rivers come together to form the Ohio River. Shippensburg was to serve as a supply base.

Major General Edward Braddock marched out of Philadelphia and advanced to within eight miles of Fort Duquesne when his force was attacked by French and Indian warriors and destroyed in early July 1755. His defeat left western Pennsylvania defenseless and unprepared to fend off attacks by enemy raiding parties, which launched a terror campaign against the isolated farms and settlements of Cumberland County. For the first time in fifty years, the reach of westward expansion retreated as refugees flocked to the roads heading east. Shippensburg was directly in their path.

Three years before, in 1752, Edward Shippen III sent his son-in-law James Burd to the town to manage affairs. On November 2, 1755, Burd wrote the following to Shippen: "We are in great confusion here…The town is full of people…five or six families in a house. We are in great want of ammunition, but with what we have we are determined to give the enemy as warm as a reception as we can." It was during this time that the settlers of Shippensburg were building Fort Morris, which they named after the governor of the province. Burd told Shippen they had one hundred men working on the project "with heart and hand every day." He expected completion within fifteen days.

Fort Morris had walls two feet thick and was situated atop a rocky hill. Though strong, this could not stop the rampage that followed in close proximity to Shippensburg. On June 6, 1757, two men were murdered and five others taken prisoner by a raiding party that attacked a farm just east of where Burd's Run crosses the road between Shippensburg and Middle Spring. Just over a month later, on July 18, another band of Indians surprised laborers harvesting wheat about a mile east of the town, killing two and capturing four others. The next day, Indians raided a nearby field killing nine and capturing four other settlers. The sporadic attacks continued until November 1758 when Brigadier General John Forbes led an expedition against Fort Duquesne, prompting its surrender without firing a shot. There was a brief respite in the bloody deeds.

While the capture of Fort Duquesne put an end to the terror campaign against settlers in Cumberland County, it also planted the seed of a conspiracy that ultimately led to the Pontiac War. It was understood by friendly tribes that the British would retreat back over the mountains once they had secured the frontier from further incursions by the French and the hostile Indian tribes. Instead, the British reneged on their promise, prompting the once friendly tribes to launch in May 1763 a series of coordinated attacks against settlements in the western frontier that forced refugees to once more seek shelter in Shippensburg.

1777: Equal to Expectations

There was a place outside Carlisle largely forgotten in the annals of history, but vital to the effort to win the Revolutionary War. Though it ranks among the first of many namesakes of a founding father, George Washington thought that York, Pennsylvania, was better suited for the task. While its precise location is open to debate, few would dispute the importance Washingtonburg had as a major logistics base for the Continental army. For over six years, its tradesmen made the weapons that kept hope alive despite Indian raids on the supply lines and the schemes of Loyalists to the Crown. It was here outside Carlisle that the army opened its first school, setting in motion a legacy in military education that continues to this day as the Army War College.

"Washingtonburg suggests nothing to the general public," Dickinson College Professor Charles Himes once said about the obscurity of the name. The only mention of it in county records was in January 1779 when a group of prominent Carlisle area residents petitioned local officials to have a bridge erected over the LeTort Spring Run near where the creek intersects with present-day East High Street. Heavy wagon traffic moving between Carlisle and Washingtonburg was wearing away the creek banks, jeopardizing the safety of travelers. "It was more than simply a little suburb, with a rather pretentious name, of a half-grown village, such as Carlisle," Himes said of Washingtonburg. "It was a very busy place, for there were workshops in which were manufactured military supplies of the most varied character...The artificers were numbered by the hundreds and had their lodging and boarding houses."

This 1947 pencil sketch by Donald Beetem depicts the Hessian Guardhouse at Carlisle Barracks. *Courtesy of CCHS.*

For much of its history, Carlisle has served as a strategic transportation hub with strong ties to the military. It was first laid out in 1751 as a county seat at a crossroads where several Indian paths intersected leading in all directions through the Cumberland Valley. As the only British outpost west of the Susquehanna River, Carlisle developed into a vital supply depot in the defense of Pennsylvania against Indian attacks on the frontier. It was from Carlisle in early July 1758 that Brigadier General John Forbes launched his expedition that forced the French to abandon Fort Duquesne. On May 30, 1757, Colonel John Stanwix arrived in Carlisle to establish its first military camp as a system of breastworks located on land bounded on the east by the LeTort Spring Run, the south by North Street and on the west, northwest and north by present-day Bedford Street.

"Where was Washingtonburg?" was one of the questions liable to come up at any informal gathering of local historians, Himes told an audience on February 19, 1907. "There is more in the query than idle curiosity that attaches to a vexed question." At the time, Himes was introducing Mrs. Charles Humrich, a daughter-in-law of the late Christian Humrich, a local historian. She had gone before the Hamilton Library Association to read an unfinished paper that her father-in-law was working on in an effort to pinpoint the location of Washingtonburg. He had concluded that at least part of this base once occupied the west end of present-day Carlisle Barracks.

"Just as the name Washingtonburg has been completely lost to tradition so have all vestiges of these extensive works disappeared from the topography of the locality," Himes said. "No identifiable remains of buildings or fragments of objects have been discovered, with perhaps one interesting exception, the so-called guardhouse. The character of this stone building leaves little doubt it was built at an early date." The professor was referring to the Hessian Guardhouse, which still stands as a museum on the Carlisle Barracks campus. Legend has it that this structure was built by Hessian prisoners captured by General Washington during his raid on Trenton the day after Christmas in 1776. However, there are no records to support this story, and the only reference in documents to Hessians being brought to Carlisle states that they did not arrive until November 1777—several months after the guardhouse had been built. Also, the foundations of several early buildings were unearthed during excavations made on post between 1933 and 1938—almost three decades after Himes gave his introduction before the association.

While much of the early fighting of the Revolutionary War took place in New York and New England, the manufacture and repair of weapons and the production of gunpowder for the Continental army was concentrated in Philadelphia because of its status as a seat of government. That thinking changed during the fall of 1776, after Washington's army was defeated in New York and began a retreat through New Jersey. The threat to Philadelphia increased, prompting Congress on December 14, 1776, to authorize the construction of manufacturing facilities in York, Pennsylvania, and Springfield, Massachusetts. This decision was superseded by a December 27 directive that moved the location of the York facility to Carlisle. Local attorney James Wilson, a signer of the Declaration of Independence, lobbied for the change by writing a letter to Congress offering his assistance in establishing a facility in Carlisle.

While General Washington preferred the York location because it was remote from the front line, Congress went with Carlisle because it was just as secure, had good road access and already had buildings available for use, making its development more cost-effective. Apparently, Washington was not informed at first of this change. On January 16, 1777, the future president wrote a letter to Colonel Benjamin Flower, who was in charge of the regiment of artificers tasked with the manufacture and repair of weapons. Washington ordered Flower to report to York and construct whatever buildings were necessary, including a furnace to process metal, a mill to bore cannon and workshops large enough to accommodate forty carpenters, forty blacksmiths, twenty wheelwrights and twelve harness makers. Washington also wanted sixty artillerymen assigned to the York installation, including a captain, five lieutenants, six corporals and six bombardiers. Eventually, Washington was advised of the change of location and directed Flower to relocate his operation to Carlisle.

By April 1777, construction at Carlisle had reached the stage where Washington could request that powder and stores at Baltimore be transferred to the new facility, which became known as the Public Works. The operation was set in motion to manufacture cannon of various calibers, cannonballs and horse-drawn vehicles to mount the artillery and haul ammunition. Iron was produced at nearby furnaces at Mount Holly Springs, Pine Grove and Boiling Springs. The mountains on either side of the Cumberland Valley provided the timber necessary to make charcoal while anthracite coal from the Wilkes-Barre area was transported down the Susquehanna River by boat to Harris Ferry and then hauled in wagons to Carlisle. Prior to its occupation, Congress had authorized New York officials to remove all bells from statehouses, churches and other public buildings for shipment first to Newark, New Jersey, and then on to Carlisle in 1778, where they were to be cast into brass cannon. For whatever reason, that work was never done and the bells remained in Washingtonburg until the end of the war, when they were shipped back to New York.

The Public Works had other functions during the Revolutionary War. A group of coopers had a shop to make barrels and casks for the Department of Military Stores to hold powder and for the Commissary Department to hold whiskey and provisions of pork, beef and other supplies preserved with salt. Washingtonburg was also the site of a military hospital, a repair facility for muskets, a recruiting station for regular army regiments and a military court that held trials for deserters, spies and other military-related cases where the sentence upon conviction was often death.

The army also opened its first school at Washingtonburg where it trained artillerists on the use, repair and maintenance of cannon. "Practice must complete what speculation can only begin," General Horatio Gates said to students on April 28, 1778. "The knowledge you have gained…of the laboratory art, as well as your experiences in life, must convince you of the truth of these general positions…We shall be happy to hear, on your return to camp…that the knowledge you gained from your residence at Carlisle is equal to the expectations." This was the first in a long line of educational institutions at Carlisle Barracks that included the Army Cavalry School of Practice, the Army Medical Service School, the Army Information School, the School for Government of Occupied Areas, the Adjutant Generals School, the Chaplain School, the Military Police School, the Army Security Agent School and the present-day Army War College that trains future strategic leaders.

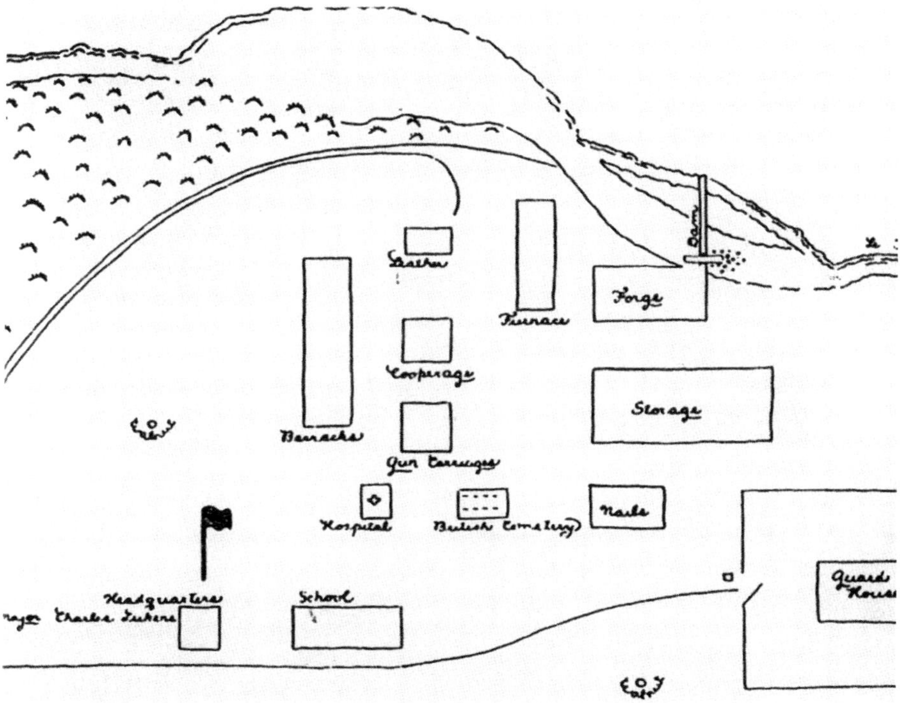

This hand-drawn map depicts the army post at Carlisle when it was known as Washingtonburg. The image is taken from the 1939 book *Military History of Carlisle and Carlisle Barracks* by Thomas G. Tousey. *Courtesy of CCHS.*

From the beginning, Washingtonburg played a major part in the war effort. Following their defeat at Saratoga in October 1777, the British intensified their campaign to draw American forces away from the main army by inciting the Indians on the frontier to make war on the settlers. This campaign led to a repeat of the same kind of atrocities that terrorized the colonists during the French and Indian War and the Pontiac War. Washington could not spare the manpower to garrison the frontier forts, so he asked Congress to raise local militia units to man the ramparts. Due to its strategic location, the Public Works at Carlisle proved vital in supplying these garrisons. The products made at the Washingtonburg facility also helped to reequip the Continental army during its difficult winter and period of reorganization at Valley Forge from late 1777 to early 1778. That year, more of the burden fell on Carlisle to manufacture arms and ammunition because the arsenal at Springfield was too far removed from the main action to be an effective supply base.

In November 1778, a force of Loyalists and Indians launched a devastating raid on the Wyoming Valley of Pennsylvania. This prompted Washington to plan punitive strikes against the Iroquois of upstate New York in the form of expeditions set for the summer of 1779 and led by General John Sullivan and Colonel Daniel Brodhead. Preparations for these attacks intensified the activity level at Washingtonburg as workers there tried to keep pace with demand. Requisitions from Brodhead alone were enough to pack 1,200 horses with gunpowder, weapons, provisions and such other items as axes, spades, picks and canvas for tent.

British general Henry Clinton knew there were colonists in south-central Pennsylvania who were secretly loyal to the Crown. Foremost among them was William Rankin of York County, who used his position as a colonel in the local militia as a cover to recruit men to the Loyalist cause. A British deserter named Alexander McDonald helped Rankin, and together the conspirators claimed they had a force of 1,800 Loyalists ready to join the Redcoats in an operation against the Continental army. In March 1779, Rankin became aware of the Sullivan and Brodhead Expeditions. To head them off, he approached Clinton with a bold plan that included a proposed march on Carlisle by British Army forces to be executed in conjunction with a Loyalist uprising to seize Washingtonburg.

Clinton had a different strategy. Instead of a direct attack, he wanted Rankin to arrange for the sabotage of the Public Works facility. Rankin was not thrilled by the prospect because he felt the only way to arm his force of Loyalists was to capture Washingtonburg intact, not destroy it. The plan was revealed after two of McDonald's men were apprehended. This prompted Clinton to suspend all operations, effectively ending the threat of Loyalist attack or sabotage on Washingtonburg.

The irony was that Rankin's original plan might have succeeded. There was hardly any security at Washingtonburg because officials in Carlisle thought the Public Works facility was out of the reach of British forces. The arrest of the two men prompted the Continental army to station two infantry companies at Washingtonburg as a precaution. A number of Loyalists were rounded up and jailed, but Rankin managed to escape. The Patriots had in their corner Lieutenant George Stevenson, an intelligence agent tasked with monitoring the activities of Carlisle-area Loyalists who carried out acts of sabotage, stirred up discord among the drivers of supply wagons and incited inmates at the county jail to lodge formal complaints about the conditions. Much of this subversion ended after Stevenson jailed some prominent Loyalists and had their property seized. From time to time, Indian attacks disrupted the supply of iron and coal to

The garrison cannon pictured is typical of artillery used during the American Revolution. It is located at the Yorktown Redoubt display on the outdoor trail of the Army Heritage and Education Center in Middlesex Township, not far from where Washingtonburg was once located. *Photo by Joseph David Cress.*

Washingtonburg, but a system was developed to keep wagon masters informed of potential hazards.

By 1780, the Carlisle area had peaked as a provider of military supplies. Economic conditions combined with counterfeiting by the British caused skyrocketing inflation that made it difficult for the Continental army to obtain even the most basic necessities for the soldiers. At Washingtonburg, there was evidence of low morale among the artificers. Discipline suffered, and Major Charles Lukens was relieved of duty as the first commandant of what became Carlisle Barracks. By late 1781, the Public Works no longer existed as a major supply center, and many of its functions had already been outsourced to such nearby facilities as Pine Grove Furnace, which stepped up its own production of shells and cannonballs for the war effort. Demand for military supplies dropped off sharply after the surrender of General Charles Cornwallis at Yorktown. On May 26, 1784, Congress ordered Washingtonburg to close. Two months later in July, an auction was held to sell off what remained after heavy machinery had been removed by the government and transported to Philadelphia.

1787: A Dangerous Instrument

There were warnings in the words of Robert Whitehill, language that spoke of dire consequences should we the people ever lose touch with where we came from. While a majority of Pennsylvania lawmakers favored ratifying the U.S. Constitution, Whitehill opposed its passage without a written guarantee that civil liberties would be protected. In a political career spanning five decades, Whitehill represented Cumberland County residents during one of the most formative periods of American history and yet his most enduring legacy is often overshadowed by the deeds of his contemporaries. Whitehill was the first person to write down and bring before a ratifying body ideas that became many of the Ten Amendments listed in the Bill of Rights.

Born on July 29, 1738, in present-day Lancaster County, Whitehill was influenced from an early age by his father—a blacksmith and farmer who held local office. He also drew inspiration from the teachings of Reverend Francis Allison, a fiery Presbyterian minister who viewed the pulpit as both a religious and political forum. Pioneer values and a Scotch-Irish upbringing shaped Whitehill's ideology into a platform that emphasized individualism, a dislike for Great Britain, a distrust for financial institutions and the fear of big government. His political views were in line with many of his Cumberland County constituents who long protested the failure of lawmakers to protect the frontier from Indian attacks. They were also opposed to economic policies that favored commercial interests in Philadelphia over the livelihood of farmers out west.

His first major battle for civil liberties came while Whitehill served in the Pennsylvania Assembly in March 1785. He had submitted a petition against a bill to renew the charter of the Bank of North America, which was founded in Philadelphia during the Revolutionary War. Though supporters thought of the bank as a stabilizing force in a fragile economy, Whitehill feared its influence on policy makers, especially since it operated outside the control of voters. "This enormous engine of power will dictate to the legislature what bills to pass," Whitehill said. While successful in having a paragraph-by-paragraph vote taken on the bill, he came away disappointed that none of his proposed changes were approved by a majority of the assembly.

Two years later, in the fall of 1787, Whitehill was a local delegate to the convention called by the state legislature to consider ratification of the U.S. Constitution. As their representative, he submitted a petition with the names of 750 Cumberland County residents who opposed the federal document. From the start, Whitehill objected to language that he felt would make the Supreme Court and the president too powerful and the Senate too much like an aristocracy. He thought it inappropriate for the vice president to preside over the Senate, especially when the body was voting to increase the pay of its members. Like his constituents, Whitehill wanted control to rest mostly with state and local government. He feared the Constitution gave Congress too much authority to pass laws that when carried out could swallow up "every object of taxation" and plunder states of their means of support while gradually eroding their sovereignty. He argued that safeguards be put in place to protect civil liberties from being swept aside.

"It is the nature of power to seek its own augmentation, and thus the loss of liberty is a necessary consequence of a loose and extravagant delegation of authority," Whitehill said. "National freedom has been and will be the sacrifice of ambition and power and it is our duty to employ the present opportunity in stipulating such restrictions as are best calculated to protect us from oppression and slavery…A bill of rights may be a dangerous instrument, but it is to the views and objects of the aspiring ruler and not the liberties of the citizens." This defiance by Whitehill antagonized James Wilson, a Carlisle attorney and signer of the Declaration of Independence.

A Federalist, Wilson argued that there was no need for protection under a bill of rights because the government derived its mandate directly from the people. He thought that the civil liberties handed down through the ages from the centuries-old Magna Carta would simply carry over to the new nation. Active in framing the U.S. Constitution, Wilson's main contribution was to help maximize the power of central government while ensuring the independence of the executive, legislative and judicial branches. An anti-Federalist, Whitehill believed the Magna Carta did not carry enough clout to guarantee civil liberties, so he continued his push for a bill of rights. "The country beginning in tyranny must end in despotism," Whitehill said. "We rob the people of their liberties when we establish a power whose usurpation they would not be able to counteract or resist." The two men had lengthy debates. Once after Whitehill cited what he thought were defects in the Constitution, Wilson responded with a twenty-thousand-word rebuttal that spanned two full days of convention time. "He yielded briefly and then spoke another fifteen thousand words," said Robert Grant Crist, a prominent Cumberland County historian.

This miniature of James Wilson was painted on ivory by Jean Pierre Henri Elouis. *Courtesy of CCHS.*

On December 12, 1787, Whitehill got the lectern long enough to propose fifteen amendments to the Constitution in what became known as the "Address and Reasons of Dissent of the Minority of the Convention of the State of Pennsylvania to their Constituents." This document spelled out in rough-draft form the ideas that were later used to formulate the Bill of Rights. Specifically, language in the address influenced the Fourth Amendment, prohibiting unreasonable searches and seizures; the Eighth Amendment, prohibiting excessive bail and cruel and unusual punishment; the Fifth Amendment right to remain silent and to be protected against double jeopardy; and the Sixth Amendment right to a speedy criminal trial before an impartial jury. In many ways, the Bill of Rights was an edited-down version of what the dissent address first proposed. Take for example, the First Amendment, which reads in part, "Congress shall make no law respecting the establishment of religion, or prohibiting the free exercise thereof, or abridging the freedom of speech, or of the press..." Now compare that with the language in the address:

> *The right of conscience shall be held inviolable; and neither the legislative, executive nor judicial powers of the United States shall have the authority to alter, abrogate, or infringe any part of the Constitution of the several states, which provide for the preservation of liberty in matters of religion.*
>
> *The people have a right to freedom of speech, of writing and publishing their sentiments, therefore, the freedom of press shall not be restricted by any law of the United States.*

Another example can be seen in the Second Amendment, which reads, "the right of the people to keep and bear arms, shall not be infringed." Here again, compare the final version to what was in the dissent address: "That the people have a right to bear arms for the defense of themselves and their states, or the United States, or for the purpose of killing game; and no law shall be passed for disarming the people or any of them, unless for crimes committed, or a real danger of public safety."

On December 12, 1787, convention delegates voted 46–23 in favor of ratifying the Constitution. The "nays" included Whitehill and all those representing Cumberland County. The Federalist majority not only rejected the notion of a bill of rights but also decided to omit from convention minutes all references to the proposal. Seeing the propaganda value, Whitehill pushed to have each delegate record the reason for his vote. "It will be a barren document otherwise," he said of the U.S. Constitution. "The public has a right to know the principles upon which delegates proceed. It is the right of every man who is bound by his vote to be permitted to explain it." This request for transparency was turned down by the majority. Even after the Constitution was ratified, Whitehill continued the fight to have a bill of rights included. His ideas were published by the anti-Federalist party and circulated in other states where leaders were persuaded by his argument for a written guarantee. The Bill of Rights was later adopted in 1791.

The political climate of the 1790s prevented a radical like Whitehill from getting reelected to the state assembly. Instead, he devoted considerable time to his farm, which was one of the largest in Cumberland County. Ironically, Whitehill and Wilson were practically neighbors. While Wilson received the valuable Lowther Manor plantation, which fronted the Susquehanna River and flanked the main road from Harris Ferry to Carlisle, Whitehill owned about 213 acres behind Wilson. Politics changed, and Whitehill was again elected to office, serving in the state House of Representatives from 1797 to 1801 and then the state Senate from 1801 to 1805.

This sketch of the Robert Whitehill house was drawn by Dorothy Kendall. *Courtesy of CCHS.*

While a senator, Whitehill was elected speaker at a time when his party sought to reform the judiciary by replacing a system based on common law with one based on statutory law. Common law uses technical terms and Latin understandable only to those with legal training while statutory law is readable by all. Radicals such as Whitehill also pointed to abuses in judicial power by the Federalists as proof that both the salaries and tenures of judges should be altered. In 1805, county residents elected Whitehill as their representative to Congress. From 1810 to 1813, the state Congressional delegation numbered eighteen representatives, fourteen of whom were Democratic Republican, the party of Whitehill and Presidents Thomas Jefferson and James Madison. As such, Whitehill's radical beliefs were somewhat tempered, and he became more of a party loyalist leading up to the War of 1812. Whitehill died at his home in present-day Camp Hill on April 4, 1813.

In his writings, Robert Crist noted several reasons for why history neglected Whitehill. For one thing, he walked the streets of Philadelphia with such titans of American history as Thomas Jefferson, John Adams, Benjamin Franklin and George Washington. Their deeds eclipsed his and tended to be covered more closely by the newspapers of the day. There is also a scarcity of original letters and documents written by Whitehill, Crist said. That said, Whitehill maintained his popularity among county residents who first voted him into the Assembly from 1776 to 1778 and then again from 1783 to 1787. Whitehill also served on the state executive council from 1779 to 1781.

1789: This Untimely Fate

Venus shined conspicuous as Rachel Wall stole her way aboard a ship docked at the wharf in the spring of 1787. In her alleged confession made two years later and only hours before her death by hanging, the Carlisle-area native described how the heavenly body featured prominently in the night sky over Boston.

The door unlocked, she easily entered the cabin where the captain and his mate lay asleep in their bed. "I hunted about for plunder and discovered under the captain's head a black silk handkerchief containing upwards of thirty pounds in gold crowns and small change," the lady pirate recalled. "I immediately seized the booty which I spent freely in company as lewd and wicked as myself."

Facing execution, the twenty-nine-year-old woman never put the blame for her downfall on her Christian upbringing, but on the schemes of her husband. Indeed, she confessed herself guilty of a "great many crimes, such as Sabbath-breaking, stealing, lying, disobedience to parents and almost every other sin a person could commit, except murder." She later added, "The many small crimes that I committed, are too numerous to mention in this sheet, and therefore a particular narrative of them…would serve to extend a work of this kind to too great a length."

With the end so near, her motives seemed pure at heart and laden with such remorse it formed the basis of her confession. "Without doubt the ever curious public will be anxious to know every particular circumstance of the life and character of a person in my unhappy situation," she said. Wall began her story by describing her early years and the piety of her father. The condemned woman then touched on her relationship with George Wall, the man who would ultimately lead her to Boston, where she was executed on October 8, 1789, for highway robbery. It is believed she was the last woman hanged in Massachusetts.

"I…was born in the town of Carlisle…in the year 1760, of earnest and reputable parents," Wall said. "They gave me a good education and instructed me in the fundamental principles of the…religion and taught me the fear of God…If I had followed the good advice [I] should never have come to this untimely fate…My father was of a very serious and devout turn of mind, and always made it his constant practice to perform family prayers in his house every morning and evening." It was also customary for her father to gather the whole family on Sunday nights to read scripture and other religious texts. After which, her father would quiz Rachel, her three brothers and two sisters on the lessons of the day's reading.

The specifics on what happened next depends on what story you want to believe. Rachel Wall is something of a folk legend with the common thread being that she married George Wall over the objections of her mother. In one version of her story, Rachel was sixteen years old when she took a trip to Harris's Ferry, present-day Harrisburg, to attend the funeral of her grandfather. There, while wandering the docks, she met a shady fellow named George. One source identified him as a fisherman and former privateer who served during the Revolutionary War.

In her confession, Rachel explained how she left her parents at a very young age and returned to stay with them for two years before leaving again. She then eloped with George to Philadelphia, where she stayed for some time before spending three months in New York. While the stories agreed the couple ended up in Boston, there are different takes on how Rachel became a pirate. One version was that George had deserted her only to return several months later with plundered treasure. He showed Rachel the booty and managed to convince her to become a pirate. In a different version, she became a maid while George took a job as a fisherman. After he returned from his first voyage, the couple partied with some friends but ended up destitute. Strapped for cash, the husband and wife turned to a life of crime after borrowing or stealing a ship at Essex.

In her confession, Rachel explained how she became a servant after George had left her and led a contented life until he returned and "enticed me to…take to bad company." While Rachel is best known for her exploits as a pirate, she made no mention of piracy in her confession. Aside from the

1787 robbery already mentioned, Rachel confessed to sneaking onboard a different vessel one night in 1789 and stealing a silver watch hanging over the head of the sleeping captain. She also made off with a pair of silver buckles from his shoes. That same year, she was arrested and convicted of robbing a woman on the streets of Boston. In declaring her innocence, Rachel claimed she was home that evening and that the eyewitness was clearly mistaken.

As for her career as a pirate, the story goes that Rachel was involved with a band of cutthroats who hunted primarily around the Isles of Shoals off the coast of Maine and New Hampshire. Their modus operandi was to anchor near an island during a storm and then rig their vessel to appear as though it would founder before setting it adrift. Rachel would scream for help at the approach of another ship, luring that crew in to be slaughtered by her fellow pirates, who would then steal all the valuables and sink the rescuing ship. This ended in September 1782 when a storm battered their pirate ship and broke the mast. It is said that George and his accomplices were swept into the ocean and drowned, leaving Rachel as a sole survivor to be rescued and returned to Boston.

However, this story conflicts with her confession, which mentions her role in the attempted jailbreak of her husband in 1785, three years after he supposedly drowned. Rachel explained how she had enclosed a file into a loaf of bread that had been handed to George by an unsuspecting jailor. George was discovered before he could make his escape. She finished her confession by thanking the local clergymen who comforted her spiritually as she awaited her execution. Her last words were: "Into the hands of almighty God I commit my soul, relying on His mercy, through the merits and meditations of my redeemer, and die an unworthy member of the Presbyterian Church."

1833: Tramps Abroad

Why must every "happily-ever after" end in tragedy born of mischief? That was the question that bugged Lucy Baird about her father—a world-renowned naturalist and early organizer of the Smithsonian Institution. She knew he was only being playful when he used his fertile imagination to weave fantastic tales for her amusement. A typical story by Spencer Fullerton Baird involved a hero and heroine who ended up getting married after surviving a perilous journey through a combination of skill, ingenuity and the timely intervention of good fairies. "One thing only I disapproved," Lucy wrote in her memoirs. "He could never be induced to stop there…in spite of all my attempts at interruption." Something bad always happened, like the couple falling into a boiling vat and being made into soap.

Hers was not a typical childhood. "A favorite playmate was a large black snake, so long that when I was mounted on the shoulder of my tall father, the snake's tail touched the ground," Lucy wrote. Known simply as "The Prof" by his Dickinson College students, Baird was convinced mankind's fear and loathing of snakes had no basis in nature and was only something adults taught children from an early age. "The whole family received strict orders that on no account was I to be in any way prejudiced against the crawling members of the animal kingdom," Lucy wrote. "Harmless snakes were given to me to play with." She grew up comfortable around serpents.

For a time, her biologist father went through a phase where he studied snakes in detail. He kept the slithering reptiles alive in barrels. Once a specimen escaped into the house and could not be found by Baird. He confided in Lucy's mother, Mary, who, like the girl, had no fear of nonvenomous snakes, but the couple was worried about how the grandmother would react to meeting this uninvited but harmless guest. "And it was very certain that my mother's sister-in-law…would be very much frightened at the bare suggestion that one of the snakes was…in the house," Lucy wrote. In the end, her parents chose not to say anything because they knew the chances of an encounter were slim and that the news would cause too much anxiety. Her mother later found the truant serpent coiled up behind a stove to keep warm. She joyfully picked him up and returned him to the barrel.

Like his daughter, Spencer Fullerton Baird grew up loving nature. A native of Reading, Pennsylvania, he used to go on long hikes in the countryside with his father. It was on these treks that Spencer first learned how to make observations of flora and fauna. He was ten years old when his father died in 1833 and the family moved to Cumberland County. It was in Carlisle and the surrounding area that his childhood interest in natural history matured into a lifelong passion that would lead him to Washington, D.C., and the influential role of secretary or chief executive officer of the Smithsonian Institution. There he played a key role in developing the museum collection into what became known as "America's Attic." He was also influential in convincing Congress to approve the purchase of Alaska from Russia in 1867. But all this started with a boy's fascination with nature and his journeys throughout the Cumberland Valley and beyond.

Spencer's brother William was a student at Dickinson College and took to the study of birds in the field. They often set out together in search of specimens. After William left Carlisle, he gave his younger brother money to pay for trips and textbooks on natural history. Using the town as his base, Spencer would set out on his own shooting expeditions. A successful trip would yield up to thirty bird skins—all of which he had stuffed so he could study each specimen in great detail and document its characteristics. His extensive work earned the young Baird respect from other field biologists.

On June 4, 1840, when Spencer was seventeen years old, he wrote a letter to famed naturalist John James Audubon about two flycatchers that he could not identify. It turned out that the boy had discovered a new species of bird. "Although you speak of yourself as being a youth, your style and the descriptions you have sent me prove to me that an old head may time to time be found on young shoulders," Audubon wrote back. Within a year, Baird would disagree with Audubon about the description of another bird species, but this only reinforced Audubon's confidence in the ability of his young colleague. When Spencer turned nineteen, Audubon gave him most of his bird collection in exchange for the youth agreeing to collect mammals the veteran biologist wanted.

By age seventeen, Spencer had graduated from Dickinson College but continued his education over the next five years through a combination of frequent trips into the countryside and book learning during inclement weather. The many years of physical conditioning enabled Baird to go far and fast without tiring. It is said that one morning he left Carlisle at 5:30 only to arrive in Manchester, Maryland, less than twelve hours later after covering a distance of about forty-two miles. The next morning, Baird woke up at about 6:30 and arrived in Baltimore by 3:00 p.m., clocking in a total of eighty miles in less than two days of travel. For years, he logged in over two thousand miles annually while carrying a knapsack, a double-barreled gun and up to forty pounds of excess weight. No wonder some of the fondest memories Lucy had of her father are tied to his travels:

> *In his tramps abroad I've heard my father say that he adopted a regular length of step, three steps to a rail of an ordinary post and rail fence…As he went along his quick eyes noted all the features of the country through which he passed and he stopped constantly to pick up plants, minerals or shoot birds. At the end of a long dusty walk, laden with these treasures, he would gradually come to present the appearance of a tramp.*
>
> *I have heard him say that on one of his walking tours he visited a little town on the interior of the state for the purpose of having a talk with the governor of Pennsylvania who, was at a hotel there. My father went into the office and asked for a room; the clerk…*[on seeing] *the dusty stranger, laden with very odd baggage, gave him a small room in the part of the house reserved for the humblest guests. My father with characteristic modesty, meekly took the quarters assigned him, went upstairs with his luggage, washed and dressed, came downstairs where he met the governor in the office receiving a hearty and a friendly greeting. The clerk at his earliest possible moment told him he had a better room now vacant and suggested that he should move.*

An earlier memory was of meeting her father at a railroad station after a long period of separation. What stood out in Lucy's mind was that he sported a beard. "As a young man, he shaved completely not even wearing a mustache," she wrote. "His hair was very dark brown and straight, but his beard was decidedly sandy in color. His eyes were a rather dark, clear grey. In his youth and early middle life, he was slender, but later he grew stout."

Lucy had gone to the station with her mother, Mary, who had passed down other stories. As a couple, Lucy's parents had come a long way. While Mary had no interest in natural history, she was supportive and always looking in on what Spencer was up to.

When her parents were courting, her father was busy with his college work. After they became engaged, Spencer wanted to spend his evenings with Mary but also had to keep up with his studies. "So he fell into the habit of taking a book with him in order that he might…still have the pleasure of sitting in the room with her," Lucy wrote. "Being an early riser and often taking long walks with his class making collections, my father would be apt to grow drowsy towards the end of the evening and…fall asleep over his book." When the hour arrived, Mary would wake him and send him home. On one occasion, her parents were walking together in the countryside when they came upon a little stream with some curious looking fish. Spencer wanted specimens but lacked a net, so Mary lent him her bonnet for him to catch the "finny treasures," Lucy wrote.

At age twenty-two, Baird became a professor of natural history at Dickinson College but also taught chemistry, physiology and mathematics. It is believed that he may have been the first faculty member to take students out on field trips. The approach soon evolved into regular Saturday excursions during which students had to hustle to keep up with their energetic mentor. Popular among his students, Baird inspired many to pursue careers in science, Lucy said. She added that these "outdoor rambles" not only resulted in specimens for the collection, but the boys also gained "practical knowledge from Nature herself." Often, each field trip ended with the students being invited over to the Baird home for some tea.

Spencer Fullerton Baird, circa 1850. *Courtesy of Dickinson College Library and Information Services.*

Over the years, Baird expanded his range to include longer trips into more distant regions of Pennsylvania, Ohio, New York and Virginia. In 1842 alone, he collected about 650 bird skins representing 128 species. His interest went beyond natural history to other areas of science to include experiments in electricity and early photography and the detailed analysis of iron ore extracted from the Pine Grove area of South Mountain. In 1848, Baird was the recipient of the first grant ever issued by the Smithsonian Institution. He used the seventy-five dollars to explore caves near Carlisle and throughout Pennsylvania in search of new animal species.

By age twenty-seven, Baird had collected 3,500 bird skins along with specimens of skulls, skeletons, embryos and reptiles. Even before his 1850 appointment as assistant secretary, Baird pushed for the Smithsonian Institution to grow beyond its roots as a research facility and become a museum. In a letter to Professor Joseph Henry, the organization's first secretary, Baird outlined a goal of making the institution "eminent above all over others...for the value of its vertebrate fossil remains...The collections I have already made...far outweigh all others of a similar character in all American collections combined," Baird wrote. On October 2, 1850, Baird left Carlisle for his new career as an administrator in Washington. For the train ride south, he had workmen load two freight cars with about eighty-nine thousand pounds of specimens.

Baird served as assistant secretary from 1850 to 1878, during which time he played a key role in getting Congress to realize the potential natural resources of Alaska. Though Baird never visited the Northwest Territory, he supervised field agents who were collecting information on its natural history and resources. Charles Sumner, a senator from Massachusetts, was chairman of the Committee on Foreign Relations and supported the purchase of Alaska from Russia as proposed by Secretary of State William Seward. The prestige that Baird carried as a scientist prompted Sumner to call on him to attend five conferences with top government officials between March 30, 1867, when the treaty was received, and April 9, 1867, when it was ratified by the Senate. In making a speech in support of the purchase, Sumner leaned heavily on the research material gathered by Baird and his agents.

It turned out that ratification of the treaty was the easy part. Supporters like Sumner had a harder time convincing the U.S. House of Representatives to pass the appropriation bill to pay for the purchase. From April 10 to May 24, 1867, Sumner asked Baird to collect even more material for a final copy of his speech. Often called "Seward's Folly," the purchase of Alaska was opposed by many House members who saw its $7.2 million price tag as too much of an expense for a country already heavily in debt from the Civil War. Others thought it better to develop the natural resources of other sparsely populated areas out west. The tide started to turn in support of the appropriation bill after Nathaniel Banks, chairman of the House Committee on Foreign Affairs, quoted Baird on the suitability of Alaskan timber to construct fishing vessels and on reports about the multitude of fish in waters off the coast. The final amended bill was passed by the House on July 23, 1869. It was agreed to by the Senate and signed by President Ulysses S. Grant four days later. As assistant secretary of the Smithsonian Institution, Baird also pioneered the study of fish cultures and persuaded Congress in 1871 to establish the U.S. Commission of Fish and Fisheries. This agency is now part of Fish and Wildlife Services.

From 1878 until his death in 1887, Baird served as secretary of the Smithsonian Institution. In his thirty-seven years with the organization, he developed an extensive network of naturalists, explorers and amateur collectors who traveled the world and braved the elements to gather up hundreds of thousands of new specimens for the national collection in Washington. On Baird's watch, the collection grew from about six thousand to over two million specimens. Through the efforts of Baird, the federal government also supported the International Exchange of Scientific Papers and established the National Museum and the National Zoological Park in Washington. Baird published extensively in the study of birds, mammals, reptiles and fish and wrote fifty thousand letters in his lifetime—a portion of which were used to maintain contact with his field agents.

1838: Mobocracy

Charles Bingham Penrose had little doubt on the outcome had he stayed inside the capitol building in Harrisburg. "They were ready to drench the chamber in blood," the Carlisle man recalled. For hours, he endured the unruly mob that disrupted state senate proceedings that dreary afternoon of December 4, 1838. Tempers flared as threats of violence stirred the crowd that gathered in the gallery, on the floor and in the lobby outside. The session began at three o'clock when the dim light of an overcast sky barely illuminated the interior. Before the night was over, Penrose would be ducking out a back window and running for his life from the chaos of partisan politics.

"I took the chair of speaker and called the body to order," Penrose would later explain in defense of his conduct. "Not long after…it became so dark that it was necessary to light the lamps in the chamber. As the light of day declined…the spectators…became more turbulent and interrupted the proceedings. These symptoms of tumult were repressed, but it soon became obvious…there was in the gallery a large body of men…who possessed the physical power and inclination to compel the senate to act according to their will. After the lamps were lighted and the night had set in, the turbulence of these people increased with the surrounding darkness. They clapped, they shouted and hissed. I endeavored in vain to preserve order."

Tensions ran high that day in Harrisburg after hundreds of men jammed the state capital amid a dispute over returns from Philadelphia following the October election. On the morning of December 4, the state house had split itself into two

This engraving of Charles B. Penrose was from the 1876 book *Men of Mark of Cumberland Valley, PA* by Alfred Nevin. *Courtesy of CCHS.*

factions over the controversy of which party—Democrat or Whig—should have majority rule. Crowds representing each side followed the action over to the senate to lend their weight in numbers to the outcome. Democrat Charles Brown was a candidate from Philadelphia whose election to the senate was in dispute. When Brown asked if he could speak, Penrose, a Whig, would not yield the floor to him. This only made a bad situation worse. "On this refusal, they filled the chamber with cries of 'Hear him…hear him…' and 'Go on, Brown, go on' and mingled their exclamations with cries of blood," Penrose said of the crowd. "They threatened the assassination of the speaker and others."

It was widely believed among Democrats that Penrose was involved in a scheme by the Whig party to defraud Pennsylvania voters of their rights and to distort the election results from key Philadelphia precincts that showed that the Democrats had won the majority of seats. The stakes were high in this power struggle to influence the complexion of state government. This bitterness would linger on into future generations. In 1882, the *American Volunteer*, a Carlisle newspaper with Democratic leanings, published a five-part series describing the role Cumberland County played in what history would call the Buckshot War. The name came from the ammunition issued to militia troops who were rushed to Harrisburg.

In the series, the newspaper stated that Penrose, a Carlisle attorney, was a "skilled manipulator of politics" who, though elected as a Democrat representing Cumberland County, "turned his back upon the shrine of Democracy to worship the golden calf of the United States Bank," which he had helped to re-charter as a state institution. Following that decision, Penrose sided more with the Whig party, drawing the ire of former supporters. He was reelected to the state senate as a Whig in 1837 and cast in the role of villain in the 1838 conspiracy. Three years later, in 1841, Penrose was appointed solicitor of the U.S. Treasury by President Harrison. He held onto this post through the end of the Tyler administration in 1845. But on December 4, 1838, Penrose was in the midst of escalating tensions within the senate chamber.

"I continued in the chair as speaker…between two and three hours during which time I made every effort to suppress the disturbances which have fixed so deep a stain on the reputation of our state," Penrose recalled. "I left it [the chair] when the senators who still remained, yielding to the apprehension of bloodshed…agreed to permit the individual…to make a speech." In a move that Penrose thought was degrading, the senate approved a motion by Democrat William T. Rodgers, a highly respected lawmaker from Bucks County. Brown addressed the chamber, but his words did more to incite the mob than to calm it down. "They replied with a loud voice that they were ready to drench the chamber in blood," Penrose said of the crowd. "They obtained control…and several members of the house and many senators escaped by the windows opposite to the entrance…" At that point, Penrose approached Rodgers hoping the Democrat could help. "I had confidence of his knowledge of the rules of order and believed him to be concerned for the honor of the senate," Penrose recalled. "I hoped that his known party connection would enable him to exert an influence more powerful than any I could employ."

Friends approached Penrose to warn him of threats that they had heard amid the crowd. Convinced that his life was in danger, they urged him to escape through a small room behind the speaker's chair and out through a back window. A ladder was placed against the wall and down Penrose went, but he was spotted by some in the crowd. "I had scarcely withdrawn until the window was surrounded by some seven or eight men uttering the most atrocious threats of vengeance," Penrose recalled. "Finding that I had escaped, they commenced a pursuit, from which I was fortunately sheltered by the darkness of the night and the shadow of one of the public buildings." It was reported that at least one man brandished a knife and threatened to kill the "scoundrels" who fled.

From the start, the *Carlisle Herald and Expositor*, the Whig newspaper in town, denounced the mob as nothing more than a pack of hired thugs from

The Pennsylvania State Capitol circa 1895. *Courtesy of CCHS.*

Philadelphia transported to Harrisburg as the muscle in a plot by Democrats to disrupt proceedings and intimidate Whig lawmakers. "Our legislative halls have become the arena of as desperate a gang of bullies, blackguards and villains as ever disgraced any country," the *Herald* reported on December 14. From the Democrat point of view, the men were patriots who caught wind of a Whig conspiracy and rallied to the capital to stand ready to meet, with force if necessary, those who would deny citizens of their rights. In its 1882 retrospective, the *Volunteer* compared the party faithful of that year to the Democrats of 1838: "They were the old guard that never surrendered... not the tame, passive creatures of whom we meet so many these days. When they found a conspiracy afoot...they showed themselves most determined and aggressive."

The *Volunteer* explained how the Democrats had their own conspiracy theory over who made up the majority of the mob. The newspaper mentioned how the administration of then governor Joseph Ritner had spent large amounts of public money in support of building railroads, canals and other infrastructure. Since Ritner was a Whig, the presumption was that this money was being paid to contractors, engineers and paymasters friendly to the Whig party. Because the 1838 election saw the defeat of Ritner, the theory went that many companies benefiting from the administration sent workers to Harrisburg to act as muscle to keep Ritner in power and to seat Whig candidates from the disputed Philadelphia precincts.

Once clear of immediate danger, Penrose notified Ritner who, in turn, issued a proclamation declaring that a lawless mob had so disrupted state government that he needed to call on militia to restore order. The *Herald* would later defend this action, saying Ritner, as commander in chief, had the constitutional power to summon the militia when an emergency arises. The newspaper sought to dispel speculation that troops were to be used as an instrument to reinforce a Whig conspiracy. "It has nothing to do with the right of members to their seats…A mob has been assembled to dictate to the legislature who shall and who shall not take their places." In answer to the call, Major General Robert Patterson of Philadelphia ordered about one thousand men to march on Harrisburg, arriving at the capital on December 9. In a letter back to Ritner, Patterson reassured the governor that the most important duty of every citizen soldier was to sustain the civil authority in an emergency.

Both Ritner and Penrose also addressed letters to Captain Edwin Sumner, commander of Carlisle Barracks, asking him to deploy federal troops under his command to Harrisburg to suppress what they considered to be an insurrection. Sumner refused, saying that tensions in the capital were solely the result of political differences between Whigs and Democrats. The captain felt it would be improper to put himself and his men between the two parties. This prompted Ritner and Penrose to contact President Martin Van Buren who, for much the same reasons as Sumner, refused to intervene out of fear that deploying federal troops for this purpose would lead to grave consequences. The *Volunteer* would later publish an editorial that would portray Penrose as a hypocrite in his attitude toward soldiers. "Charles the Bold of Cumberland denounced the very idea of a military stationed at the barracks. No sooner is the precious person of this valiant back window conspirator endangered…that he calls for drums and guns and muskets and bayonets and cannon…Oh Consistency, thou art a jewel…Oh Penrose, thou art a cowardly ———."

Meanwhile, the episode in the senate chamber created such an atmosphere of menace that many thought Pennsylvania was on the verge of civil war. In the days that followed, there was tension but no reports of widespread violence. On December 8, Sumner visited Harrisburg to meet with Ritner in person to explain why he refused to deploy troops. "I believe I left him satisfied of the correctness of my course," Sumner wrote in a December 9 letter. "The governor believes there is imminent danger of an immediate outbreak but I must say that I saw nothing there yesterday that led me to the same beliefs. The town was perfectly quiet, and the inhabitants were engaged in their usual pursuits without manifesting the slightest alarm."

On December 11, the *Herald* published an excerpt from a letter to the editor that the excitement in Harrisburg is "not so great at present owing to the fact that a large military force…under the command of Major General Patterson is now here…determined to suppress all notorious proceedings and uphold the supremacy of the law." The letter went on to state the appearance of this volunteer militia force has abated the "ardor of the mobocracy and caused them to be less bold." However, there was concern that although some had departed Harrisburg, there was enough of a core left behind to recruit strength and "made it another effort to uproot the institutions of our country," the *Herald* reported. In a separate letter, also published on December 11, the *Herald* reported that Harrisburg is "in great measure restored to quiet although the bullies and rowdies that compose the mob have not by any means entirely disappeared. It is thought by many that a large number…are concealed about the taverns of the suburbs of the town and are holding themselves in readiness to be called upon at any moment their leaders may deem advisable to recommence operations." Indeed, the *Herald* mentioned that while the state senate was back in session, Penrose was absent as speaker because "it is still unsafe for him to go out." On the night of December 10, someone fired a pistol at A.G. Ege after mistaking him for Penrose. A Carlisle resident, Ege was not hurt in the incident involving an unknown assailant who escaped into the darkness.

When Patterson arrived in Harrisburg, he spelled out conditions to Governor Ritner. He made it clear that he would not order his soldiers to fire on any civilians except in self-defense or protection of public property, nor would Patterson order his men to clear the capital or help either party to install leaders in the senate or House of Representatives. In its 1882 series, the *Volunteer* noted how half the soldiers under Patterson were Democrats and that they were in Harrisburg for only a week before being relieved by a battalion of troops under the command of Major General Samuel Alexander. He was in charge of the Eleventh Division of the Pennsylvania militia, which drew manpower primarily from Cumberland, Perry and Franklin Counties.

On Saturday, December 15, at around 9:00 p.m., Alexander issued orders to three militia companies from Carlisle to march to Harrisburg early Sunday morning. The companies included the Carlisle Light Artillery under

Captain E.M. Biddle, the Carlisle Light Infantry under Captain William Moudy and the Marion Rifle Corps under Captain Samuel Crop. These troops remained at the state arsenal until Saturday, December 22, when they were deemed no longer necessary and ordered to return home after tranquility was restored. In its coverage, the *Volunteer* implied that Alexander had greater sympathy for the Whig cause than Patterson. On December 20, the newspaper published the following editorial critical of Alexander and his methods as a commander:

> *This military chieftain appears determined to cover himself with some kind of notoriety at all hazards...He suddenly appears in Carlisle under the cover of night and secretly details three companies to proceed to the seat of war, without even intimating to Colonel* [Willis] *Foulk, the commander of the battalion, his intention.*
>
> *This insult to Col. Foulk and the other officers and companies of the battalion is undoubtedly a part of the premeditated plan of the conspirators at Harrisburg for the purpose of ensuring the presence of those whom they think can render the pliant instruments in driving the people into subjection.*
>
> *Although the Sabbath morning was selected for the purpose of astounding our peaceful citizens with the clang of arms and the stormy music of the drum and fife, the command when assembled consisted of but sixty men...and of these, two-thirds are sturdy Democrats, who left town hazzahing for Porter. Of these men, the people assembled at Harrisburg have nothing to fear.*
>
> *The present campaign against the people, it is said has already cost the state from $60,000 to $100,000. It is reported that these troops are to draw pay and rations for three months.*

The *Volunteer* was referring to David Porter, the Democrat who defeated Ritner by at least five thousand votes to become the new governor. It was reported Foulk was also a Democrat. A week later, on December 27, the *Herald* praised the Carlisle contingent for its dedication to duty by quoting the *Harrisburg Telegraph*: "Volunteers under better discipline are rarely if ever seen...They seem to possess in all respects every requisite to the claim and character of citizen soldier." That same day, the *Herald* quoted Alexander on comments he made about the anti-Whig conspiracy as he was dismissing his troops:

> *It cannot be denied or concealed...that great efforts have been made...to induce some of you...to swerve from the path of duty—to persuade you*

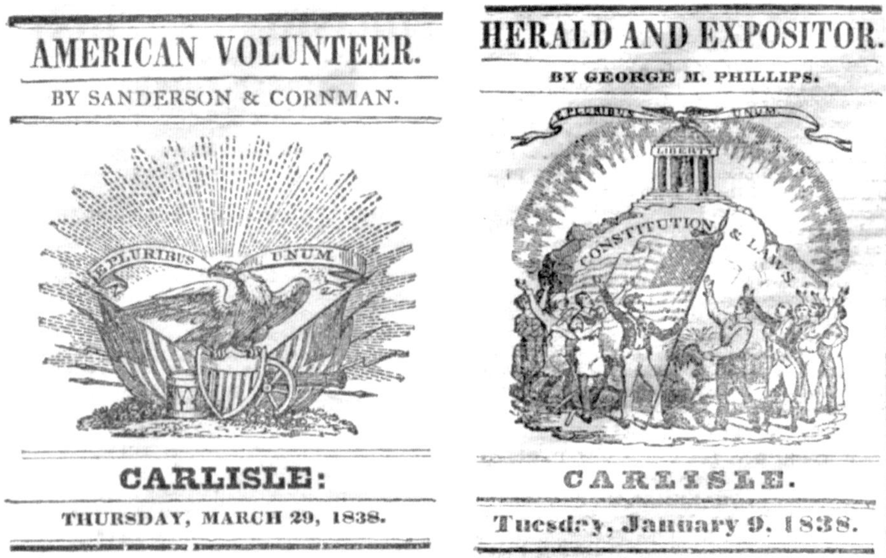

These were banners used by rival Carlisle newspapers the *American Volunteer* and the *Carlisle Herald and Expositor*. *Courtesy of CCHS.*

> *that you were called out to aid a political party instead of preserving the peace, the honor and integrity of the state. I...proclaim the failure of such efforts. They have had no effect on you. You have done your duty—you have sustained and enhanced the character of your battalion—you are called to perform the proudest duty of a citizen soldier and have responded to the call.*

In a separate article, also published on December 27, the *Herald* bashed the *Volunteer* and, more specifically, its editor, George Sanderson, for bringing up the money issue. "The greater the expenses, neighbor Sanderson, the greater should be your shame and that of other conspirators...who attempted to overthrow our government—who urged on a bloodthirsty gang of desperadoes to attempt the lives of senators—and who made it necessary for the governor to call out a militia force to protect...authorities from the outrage of the mob."

Meanwhile, the *Volunteer* took the money issue a step further in its December 27 edition when it mentioned how Alexander had instructed his troops to meet him at a local hotel to be paid. The newspaper claimed that local soldiers were promised three months of pay for their trouble but were only paid twenty-eight cents per day for a total of one dollar and ninety-eight cents. A writer calling himself "Equity" wrote an editorial entitled,

"Outrage upon Outrage," in which he described the compensation as a "miserable pittance" and a "despicable sum" for volunteers who were "forced from their homes" and "driven by the menace of a heavy fine into a course that they heavily despised."

Not to be overlooked were two militia companies from the Mechanicsburg area commanded by captains William Bigley and Jacob Dorsheimer. Shortly after Ritner's proclamation, they marched to Harrisburg to offer their service, but had no specific orders or instructions from either a commanding general or a colonel. Alexander intercepted these two companies before they could report to Ritner and promptly ordered them out of town. In its 1882 series, the *Volunteer* speculated that the reason why this was done was because both companies were comprised mostly of Democrats. Alexander gave the company commanders until sundown to comply with the order to withdraw or they would be arrested. The companies retreated back over the Susquehanna River, stacked their weapons on the grounds of a nearby hotel and returned to the shore to view Harrisburg from the west bank.

In the span of one week, both Carlisle newspapers published editorials entitled "The Crisis" to demonize the opposition party and rally supporters to their cause. On December 14, the *Herald* reported that some Cumberland County residents "made themselves notorious by their talking and swaggering and did many things that we trust, in…moments of sober reflection, they would be…ashamed of." In emphasizing its point, the *Herald* quoted the following excerpt from a Philadelphia newspaper:

> *The most extraordinary language has been…uttered in the halls of legislation, allowed and unchecked. One man, apparently an Irishman, said to be a lawyer from Carlisle, loudly proclaimed that the law was over…That the holy law now in force was the law of God Almighty as brought into the world by every man!—meaning physical force!! Such doctrines are uttered in…places that should be sacred to the laws and the constitution.*

Six days later, on December 20, 1838, the *Volunteer* published its own rendition of "The Crisis" in which it described how the greed of the Bank of America was tied to the alleged plot by Penrose and others to sidestep elections:

> *Since…the Revolution, a change has come over the spirit and character of people…a grasping, ever-reaching disposition to amass wealth has assumed the place of that Republican simplicity and noble daring which prompted the deeds of our ancestors…The palsied arms of avarice is suspended*

continually over our legislative halls, threatening the representatives of the people who are faithful to their trust…and seductive allurements of pleasure…are proffered freely to those who would bow down and worship at the shrine of Mammon.

This attempt is the last in a series of plots and stratagems of bankers, brokers and lottery vendors who, having grown desperate from defeat at the polls are trying to annul popular elections and violate the constitution that they may still further glut their avarice.

We say to the people of Cumberland County wake up, arouse and prepare to defend the dearest rights of free men. Time passes…One week hence and it may be too late. The conspirators may then have their foul designs against your rights and liberties carried into effect.

The crisis has now arrived. The capital…is a garrisoned town—a thousand troops have been paraded on the banks of the noble river that waters the shore of your own county, and from your own hills you may witness the gleam of arms and hear the roll of drums…This is not a dream—You are not free. Tomorrow you may be slaves.

In a separate article, also published on December 20, the *Volunteer* reported how a committee of Democrats had met at the Cumberland County Courthouse on December 18 where they passed a series of resolutions. Among them was a claim that the Whig party had filed fraudulent returns declaring their candidates had been elected by a majority. The Democrats also accused the Whigs of backing up their tyranny with large numbers of soldiers and artillery to force the public into obedience. While Democrats praised the crowd for its "bold and fearless stand…in defense of the constitution," they condemned the march of troops from Cumberland County into Harrisburg on the Sabbath. In response, the *Herald* belittled the importance of this Democratic committee and its resolutions in the following editorial:

This speaks well for all parties in our community and shows the impossibility of…designing demagogues seducing the virtuous and peaceable citizens from the path of duty…After circulating the most inflammatory handbills—after the most disgusting falsehoods being published in The Volunteer *and the strongest appeals to the worst passions of the human heart, no more than sixty persons including spectators attended* [the committee meeting] *in a county of 35,000.*

The design of the meeting was to cover the outrages committed at Harrisburg, to give the conduct of this mob the character of patriotic citizens,

> *peaceably assembling to resist the invasion and destruction of their rights and...to give a few malignant men here an opportunity of venting their spleen upon the head of some of the best and the most deserving statesmen in our commonwealth. Happily...it turned out to be a ridiculous farce.*

Eventually a resolution was reached where the faction led by Democrat William Hopkins gained control of the statehouse. That faction had a majority of duly elected members. As for the senate, it remained a coalition of both parties. In January 1839, Cumberland County Democrats pushed to have a special election held even as they called on Penrose to resign. To the *Volunteer*, Penrose staying in office was both an insult to the intelligence of his constituents and proof that the embattled senator was willing to "sink his character as a public man still lower, if possible, in the abyss of...disgrace." Penrose issued a writ for the special election to be held on January 15, the same day Democrat David Porter was scheduled to be inaugurated as governor.

The timing only added to the outrage. The *Volunteer* saw it as a ploy by Penrose to reduce voter turnout among Democrats by forcing them to choose between going to the polls and attending the inauguration. In an editorial entitled "The Sublimation of Meanness," the newspaper challenged the party faithful not to fall for the scheme but to exercise their right to vote. "They will be content with the reflection that on some other day they can be called upon to pay their respects to the chief magistrate of our redeemed commonwealth," the editorial reads. "We are certain your course will...make this last act of meanness recoil on the heads of its authors." If indeed it was a ploy, it backfired. Penrose did not appear on the special ballot, and the Whig party candidate lost to Democrat Thomas C. Miller by a vote of 5,041 to 4,813 among residents of Cumberland, Franklin and Adams Counties.

Despite tradition, Ritner was denied a place as retiring governor in the inauguration procession to the capitol. Though viewed with bane and ridicule during the Buckshot War, Ritner left behind an important legacy as a single-term governor who supported free public education for every child. When state lawmakers tried to repeal the Free School Act of 1834, Ritner lobbied to keep the law in effect with help from State Representative Thaddeus Stevens. Prior to that, few but the wealthy and elite could afford a quality education for their children. In his last annual message to Pennsylvania residents, Ritner mentioned that when he took office in 1835, the state had 762 common schools and seven academies. By the end of his only term

This photo by John Choate depicts the October 15, 1902 dedication ceremony of the Ritner Monument at the Mount Rock Methodist Churchyard. *Courtesy of CCHS.*

as governor, there were 5,000 common schools, thirty-eight academies and seven female seminaries.

A Berks County native, Ritner was born on March 25, 1780, to parents who had little interest in providing their children with an education. Despite that, Ritner sought out ways to learn. At age thirteen, he was interested in becoming a farmer. His father hired him out as a farmhand to Jacob Myers, a farmer near Churchtown in present-day Monroe Township. Myers was so impressed by Ritner that he took the young man with him when he moved to a farm near Newville. In May 1801, Ritner married Susan Alter, the daughter of a well-to-do farmer. Eventually, Ritner moved to his brother-in-law's farm in Allegheny County. He would later be elected seven times to the state legislature before becoming a governor. After his term ended, Ritner purchased a farm at Mount Rock south of Newville, where he lived until his death on October 19, 1869, at age ninety.

Though he left office amid turmoil, Ritner has since been recognized for his achievements. In 1901, state lawmakers allocated funds to erect a marker at his grave in the Evangelical Church cemetery at Mount Rock. On July 8, 1938, the *Sentinel* reported how many Carlisle area residents and county officials supported a proposal to rename the reconstructed Chambersburg Pike between Carlisle and Shippensburg the Ritner Highway, which it is still known as today.

1840: This Lovely Earth

Farmers had arrived by the bushel that summer day in 1840 in eager anticipation of witnessing failure. Frederick Watts had announced that he would demonstrate on his farm north of Carlisle some newfangled contraption for harvesting wheat. Locals were so skeptical of the practicality of the machine they dubbed it "Watts' Folly." Others were downright distressed by the notion that the McCormick Reaper could one day put a lot of men out of work. Sources reported between five hundred and one thousand spectators had gathered around the twelve-acre field waiting for Watts, a gentleman farmer, to begin his downfall.

A Carlisle native, Watts took up position behind the horse-drawn cutter bar, reel and platform. His part in the process was to rake the grain off so it could be bound into bundles later. "The wheat stood tall. The team was started, the cutting was excellent," Watts would later recall. "The draught was not very heavy, but the general decision was that one man could not remove the wheat rapidly enough from the machine. The team could not be driven more than ten or twelve rods till it was necessary to stop and rest the raker and straighten up his sheaves." It seemed at first the skeptics had good reason to doubt the labor-saving potential of such a mechanism. Watts recalled how help arrived at a crucial moment to save the demonstration:

> *A well-dressed gentleman of ordinary size and pleasant demeanor came up and asked whether he might be permitted to remove the wheat for a few rounds. Being answered in the affirmative, he mounted the machine and*

> *took the raker's stand. With perfect ease he raked off the wheat nor did he seem to labor hard. After two or three rounds, the spectators reversed their formal decision and unanimously agreed that the machine was a complete success. "Watts' Folly" became a favorite and thus was introduced into the Cumberland Valley. The well-dressed gentleman who did the raking was Cyrus H. McCormick, the inventor of the American Reaper.*

The timely arrival of this champion of innovation was not a total surprise. Cyrus McCormick had roots in Cumberland County. His grandfather, Thomas McCormick, owned a farm along the Conodoguinet Creek near Hogestown in present-day Silver Spring Township. This property remained in the possession of the Harrisburg branch of the McCormick family from about 1745 until May 1983 when the surviving trustees donated the Home Farm to the Natural Lands Trust Inc., a nonprofit organization committed to preserving historically significant land. The trust added a deed covenant guaranteeing that nearly 85 percent of the property would be preserved as agricultural in perpetuity. A marker explaining this history sits along the Carlisle Pike.

This roadside marker along Route 11 in Silver Spring Township shows the location of the McCormick Home Farm. *Photo by Joseph David Cress.*

Despite the successful demonstration, the McCormick Reaper did not catch on at first among farmers in Pennsylvania and nationwide. Only three thousand of these machines were made in 1850. Ultraconservative farmers were prejudiced against the Reaper because it would replace human workers. There were cases where these machines had to be locked away to prevent farm workers from destroying them. In 1840, the preferred method to harvest wheat was the sickle and crop production was limited by a shortage of trained laborers. The Civil War made this shortage even more severe driving a need for labor-saving devices. By 1865, opposition to the Reaper had virtually disappeared and it had become standard equipment on most farms. The Reaper was not the first time Frederick Watts was ahead of the curve in agricultural reform.

"About the middle of June 1839, I was driving in a carriage with my wife from New York to Philadelphia," Watts recalled. "Near Trenton, New Jersey, I was met on the road by a former resident of Carlisle Barracks, Lieutenant William Inman…who invited us to spend the night at his house on the farm. We went over. The next day he showed me a field of beautiful wheat which was rapidly ripening for the harvest. He told me that two years prior…he had procured three bushels of the seed near Leghorn, Italy and was now raising his second crop. I obtained from him six barrels of the same kind and sowed it on my farm near Carlisle…From the six barrels…it was spread through the Cumberland Valley and into other portions of the state." Watts had introduced into Pennsylvania a Mediterranean variety of wheat that matured early enough to escape severe damage from the Hessian fly, a highly invasive and destructive insect.

The same farmers who ridiculed Watts for his endorsement of the Reaper would later come to honor him for his devotion to the betterment of their livelihood. Watts was a man of many titles, including "Father of Penn State" and "U.S. Commissioner of Agriculture." Three decades after the "Folly," Watts had these words for a group of Cumberland County farmers: "With regard to our occupation, we should look upon this lovely earth as the beautiful landscape of God's Creation, imbued with the powers of life…yielding its elements and products to the delicate nursing operations of your hands."

Though a love for farming was his most enduring legacy, Watts never made a living off of it. Born on May 9, 1801, in Carlisle, he was the eldest son of David Watts, a leading Pennsylvania attorney. Frederick entered Dickinson College in 1815 but did not graduate because financial problems forced the temporary closure of the school in 1819. That same year, Watts moved to Erie County, where he spent the next two years on the farm of his uncle William Miles, a leader in agriculture, politics and railroading. It was here that Watts first developed a deep appreciation for farming and the agrarian way of life. He then returned to Carlisle to study law under Andrew Carothers and was admitted to the bar in 1824.

Watts then joined Carothers in private practice in Carlisle. His strength of character, boundless energy and abiding self-confidence was evident from the start of his forty-two-year legal career. "Whatever he undertook he did with all his might and whatever he believed, he believed implicitly," Reverend Alfred Nevin wrote in his collection of biography entitled *Men of Mark of Cumberland Valley*. "He…was regarded as a man of large intellect, sterling integrity and unblemished honor. To these he added the impression of perfect belief in the justice of his cause; and this was effected in a manner which was always dignified, and in speech that was clear, strong, convincing and never tedious. He despised quirks and quibbles, was a model of fairness in the trial of a cause, and always encouraged and treated kindly younger members of the bar that he saw struggling honorably for prominence."

Judge Frederick Watts. *Courtesy of CCHS.*

Aside from being an attorney, Watts served as a reporter of state Supreme Court decisions from 1829 to 1845, personally recording over eleven thousand pages of legal proceedings. This was at a time before stenographers and typewriters, when short summaries of the findings of fact and the conclusions of law had to be derived from mass amounts of testimony and then transcribed by hand. Watts was so busy he would often spend weeks catching short catnaps of two to three hours a day on the sofa of the office where he did his work. In early March 1849, Watts was appointed president judge of the Ninth Judicial District, which included Cumberland,

Perry and Juniata Counties. In October 1851, Judge Watts, a Whig, faced stiff competition in a highly Democratic judicial district. While Watts carried Cumberland County, he lost by a majority of about four hundred votes cast by residents in Perry and Juniata Counties.

About nine months before the election, a farmers' convention was held in Harrisburg on January 21, 1851. There, delegates from fifty-five Pennsylvania counties gathered to form a state agricultural society whose main objective was to establish a school where scientific methods in agriculture would be taught. An act to incorporate the organization was signed into law that March, and Watts was elected as the society's first president. A visionary who saw the need for education reform, Watts embraced the challenge. He had repeatedly warned farmers not to enroll their sons in a traditional college setting, which emphasized the study of Greek and Latin to prepare students for careers in law, medicine and theology. In his own words, he explained the problem:

> *Our institutions of learning...are not adapted to the education of young men for the business of agriculture. The expense is too great and the character of the education they acquire unfits them to the occupation of a farmer. The body, by an uninterrupted application to books, at a period of life when the habits of a man are formed, is rendered, in a measure, incapable of labor, and the mind is trained to an inclination and course of thought ill-adapted to the practical operations of the farm.*

Like others, Watts realized the only way the United States could advance as a country was to make education affordable and relevant to the masses rather than just the wealthy elite. What he wanted was a place where farmers could send their sons and learn the practical sciences behind the art of farming. "They should be taught the English language, mathematics, geography, chemistry, botany, astronomy and such other kindred subjects," Watts said. "Certain hours of every day should be devoted to the manual labor of the farm and to the construction and use of implements. This labor, well directed, would be productive in that the institution would be in a measure sustaining. Such an institution is loudly called for."

Under Watts's leadership, the Pennsylvania State Agricultural Society pushed for legislation to incorporate a statewide Farmers High School that was approved by state lawmakers and signed into law by Governor William Bigler, a Cumberland County native, in 1854. The name was a marketing choice designed to set farmers at ease. Though called a "high school," college-level courses would be offered leading up to a baccalaureate degree. Follow-up legislation was passed in 1855 establishing a thirteen-member board of trustees of which Watts was the first president. He held that position of leadership until 1874. His first task as board president was to guide the effort to select a site for a new school.

Several proposals were reviewed, and on September 12, 1855, Watts made the motion to accept a two-hundred-acre site in Centre County as the location for the Farmers High School. There was criticism over the selection of a site that lacked running stream water and was far removed from existing rail lines. The *American Volunteer* attacked the choice with the following words: "After a long and patient search, a tract was discovered…which could not be impeached by the smallest thread of a rivulet. In this desert waste, not a spring gurgles to the surface for the relief of the weary harvester or panting herd. Here President Watts planted his agricultural farm and college." As the Democratic newspaper in Carlisle, the *Volunteer* lobbied to have the school located in Cumberland County.

Watts defended the choice: "With the approval of my associates, I could have gladly have taken it into my dear valley of Cumberland, but in the exercise of a sound and clear judgment, the board having looked over all proposed lands and considered all circumstances believe the one chosen to be the best." The site selected, Watts designed a large barn, which became the first structure to be erected on the campus. On September 2, 1857, Watts hosted a dinner meeting of the trustees during which he made a speech that further outlined his vision for the school that almost a century later would become Pennsylvania State University: "We must combine the cultivated intellect and social amenities and mental refinement with a strong practical usefulness and sound virtues of the agriculturist who, giving the sweat of his brow, receives from Providence such bounties as are now stored around us in this building and spread upon these tables, the daily support of all human life."

Watts concluded the speech with a challenge to raise the twenty-five thousand dollars in donations necessary to construct Old Main. While his words inspired those gathered to applaud and pledge their support, a financial crisis and widespread crop failure soon followed. Many of the pledges went unfulfilled and enthusiasm waned for the school. The new institution was in dire straits before it could even open. With help from others, Watts kept lobbying for the Farmers High School, and gradually economic conditions improved. Watts knew how to handle fiscal problems. In April 1841, he was elected president of the nearly bankrupt Cumberland Valley Railroad and through penny-pinching turned the business into a financial success.

When the Farmers High School opened in 1859, it charged male students sixteen years and older a fee of $100 per ten-month session. This was about one-third the average fee charged by other colleges and included not just tuition and room and board but also washing, fuel, light and books. The trustees renamed the school the Agricultural College of Pennsylvania after President Lincoln signed the Morrill Land Grant Act in 1862. Twelve years later, in 1874, it became Pennsylvania College, and in 1953, the name changed to the current Pennsylvania State University. To this day, Penn State operates a College of Agricultural Sciences.

In 1857, Watts purchased 140 acres west of Carlisle where he erected a model farm. He used this property as a platform of experimentation in which to test different fertilizers, crops, soils, farm implements and breeds of livestock. On the grounds, he constructed a bank barn that was reportedly the largest barn in Pennsylvania. It was designed to allow hot, moist air from the hay to escape in a diffused manner along the walls and under the eaves to greatly reduce the fire risk.

This 1987 photograph by M.H. Sperow shows buildings on the Frederick Watts model farm prior to demolition in 1988. The barn was built in 1867. *Courtesy of CCHS.*

The Watts model farm stayed in agriculture until 1986 when the land was purchased by Arkansas Best Freight. In February 1987, the Pennsylvania Historical and Museum Commission Bureau for Historic Preservation determined that the Watts farmstead met the criteria for nomination to the National Register of Historic Places. The completed nomination was submitted in the summer of 1988 and came within a month of final approval when ABF executives ordered the destruction of all historic structures on the property to make way for a business park. Today, a PHMC marker stands along the Ritner Highway west of Carlisle to tell the story of the model farm.

Watts also played a role on the national stage. On January 20, 1852, the Pennsylvania State Agricultural Society adopted resolutions in support of the establishment of the United States Agricultural Society of which Watts was elected as one of its vice-presidents. Throughout the 1850s, the state society lobbied Congress for the creation of a federal bureau. On May 15, 1862, Lincoln signed into law a bill that created the U.S. Department of Agriculture. When President Grant asked him to become the third U.S. Commissioner of Agriculture, Watts declined the offer at first, preferring to devote his energies at home and toward the college. Grant insisted, and friends encouraged Watts to accept the appointment, which he did in 1871.

Watts used the office as a means to promote the interest of farmers. This work included strengthening the ties between the department, agricultural societies and land grant colleges. As commissioner, Watts established the Division of Microscopy to investigate plant diseases and share information with farmers. He did this despite the fact the department suffered from a lack of funding. His experience in managing the financial woes of both the Cumberland Valley Railroad and the Farmers High School enabled Watts to do more with less.

An advocate of forestry issues, Watts pushed for regulations, and on August 15, 1876, Congress passed a bill authorizing him to appoint an agent to assess future supply and demand for timber and forest supplies. This was the start of what would later become the U.S. Bureau of Forestry. Unlike other federal agencies under the Grant administration, the Department of Agriculture under Watts was free of scandal and corruption.

After federal service, Watts returned to his home outside Carlisle, where he lived another twelve years. He died around 2:00 a.m. on Saturday, August 17, 1889. The *Volunteer* reported how Watts fell into a deep sleep Friday afternoon, and when friends tried to rouse him, they saw that he was in a comatose state. His daughter would later say, "His mind was clear, his facilities good. He was simply worn out and went quietly to sleep."

1847: That Oppressive Lawsuit

Peeking in by lantern light, Joseph Whitcomb had promised to keep quiet. He only wanted to catch a fleeting glimpse of fugitive slaves resting on piles of hay in the stable. Rumors flew wild in the neighborhood of Daniel Kaufman that he had runaways. Curious, Whitcomb ventured out with others to the Kaufman farm just outside Boiling Springs in South Middleton Township. There, they stopped at the barnyard gate to listen for any voices. It was between eight and nine o'clock on the night of October 9, 1847. Hearing no one, Whitcomb walked up to the window, looked in and saw a light in the stables. He reported it to the others.

"We opened the door and spoke to Kaufman," Whitcomb would later testify in federal court. "For a joke, I asked him if he was gearing his horses to go to York. He just laughed and said yes." Then someone asked if there were any slaves inside. At first, Kaufman denied it, but Whitcomb and company insisted on taking a peek. Kaufman finally agreed to allow it on the condition that they would tell no one. They also promised not to make any noise because the runaways were tired from their flight north and needed rest.

Opening the stable door, Kaufman led the group in by lantern to the animal stalls. "We looked over (and) counted them," Whitcomb told jurors. "There were thirteen—two men, two women and the rest children…of different sizes. The men raised up on their elbows and talked. We asked them whether they were runaways. They said they were. Their master had died and their mistress was going to sell them. They thought it was best to run off while they had a chance." Outside, Whitcomb saw how

This photograph of Daniel Kaufman at age eighty-one was published in the October 15, 1899 edition of the *Philadelphia Press*. *Courtesy of CCHS.*

the wagon was layered with straw and had its sideboards up in readiness to transport the fugitives to the next station on the Underground Railroad.

From 1835 to 1848, Kaufman was part of a network of covert agents who helped runaway slaves gain their freedom. His involvement in this conspiracy ended after the owners of the thirteen fugitives sued Kaufman to recover monetary damages on lost property. Kaufman lost in federal court and was ordered to pay about $4,000 in costs and damages. In an 1899 article by the *Philadelphia Press*, Kaufman explained the challenges faced by both the runaways and Underground Railroad conductors: "Isolated as were the slaves of the South upon large plantations, there…existed among them knowledge that the path of freedom lay in the direction of the North Star and that along that path lived men who would brave imprisonment and financial loss to help them on their way. Between most of them and freedom rolled the Potomac River."

The most favored routes of the network ran through Pennsylvania and Ohio. The mountains on either side of the Cumberland Valley formed a natural highway on which to move slaves undetected to the Northeast and beyond to Canada. In his interview with the *Press*, Kaufman mentioned the route taken by the slaves and the locations of nearby stations: "Crossing the Potomac at nightfall, the runaway slave can reach the Pennsylvania line before daylight, but would have to go in hiding until the next night to reach his friends in Chambersburg, sixteen miles from the Maryland line. There for the first time he would meet friends who would attend to his wants, and if the coast was clear, would take him the next night to Shippensburg, another station eleven miles further."

When hiding out, the fugitives hunkered down sometimes for days on end in cellars, attics and haylofts until the threat of discovery had passed. "There he would remain...until nightfall would make it safe to sally forth and reach the next station. Word being sent ahead to the agents that the fugitive was coming," Kaufman explained. To the conspirators, a station was needed at Boiling Springs because the distance from Shippensburg to Harrisburg was too great for escaping slaves to travel in one day. Situated in a remote location close to the mountains, Boiling Springs was ideal as a link in the route that took runaway slaves east from Pine Grove Furnace on South Mountain to the Susquehanna River where they crossed into Harrisburg. Being on the edge of Boiling Springs, the Kaufman farm was rather secluded, located along the millrace near the ironworks.

About a mile south of the village, there was a place called Island Grove where Kaufman sheltered slaves overnight in an abandoned log cabin. He described it to the *Philadelphia Press*: "[It] was not only densely wooded, but was...a tangled mass of green briars and all kinds of rank growth, so that rabbits could hardly run through it without knowing its paths." A nearby spring provided drinking water for the fugitives. In times of inclement weather or when it was considered safe, Kaufman would shelter the runaways in either his farmhouse or barn.

While he kept no records, Kaufman estimated at least sixty runaway slaves passed through his station during the thirteen years it operated. "From 1835 to 1848, I continued the agency here, assisting anyone who came and hauling many away after [nightfall] on wagons to the next station in Carlisle or Harrisburg," Kaufman told the *Press*. "Yet I have not heard of a single slave whom I assisted being recaptured, nor did any that had reached Canada...ever notified [notify] me of having obtained the object of their flight." The greatest number of fugitives he handled at any one time was the thirteen slaves who escaped in October 1847 from the Oliver family of Williamsport, Maryland. This group consisted of two husbands, two wives and their children who fled slavery out of concern that family members would be separated and sold farther south.

The station at Boiling Springs operated in a community that was often unsympathetic toward the plight of runaway slaves. Cumberland County in the mid-nineteenth century had more Southern leanings than Northern and had a history of substantial slave holdings. Its trade routes went south and southwest. Southerners, particularly from Baltimore, spent summers at nearby resorts. Half the students at Dickinson College were from the South along with many of the army officers stationed at Carlisle Barracks. In 1810,

This stereograph by John Choate depicts the dam at Island Grove circa 1876 to 1880. *Courtesy of CCHS.*

half the slaves in Pennsylvania were living in Cumberland County, and by 1840, there were still twenty-four slaves in residence within its borders.

All this helped to sustain the Fugitive Slave Laws and the institution of slavery. "Consequently, these men who acted as agents of the Underground

Railroad…defied not only the laws of the land but also public opinion," Kaufman said in his interview. The *American Volunteer*, a Carlisle newspaper, voiced its opinion on the Underground Railroad in the following editorial published in November 1848 during Kaufman's county court trial:

> *In the neighborhood of Kaufman's residence, there appears to be a number of the most inveterate* [persistent] *abolitionists…who aid in the escape and the secreting away of negroes. This spirit of false philanthropy receives the frown of every good citizen. Slaves have been recognized by the Constitution as property, and every sensible man…should acquiesce in the recognition. The law should not be trampled upon, and individual rights should not be depressed by a wild and dangerous fanaticism.*

The old county courthouse on the square in Carlisle was the scene of five fugitive slave cases that demonstrated the growing tensions between the North and the South. The first case was in 1832 when Thomas Anderson, a slave owner from Frederick, Maryland, petitioned the court to grant him custody of a slave named Jim who ran away in 1829. On October 31, 1832, Associate Judge William Line granted the request, and Anderson removed Jim from Carlisle and transported him to Maryland. The second case stemmed from a June 3, 1847 riot that took place in front of the courthouse during which a slave owner from Hagerstown, Maryland, was seriously injured.

Known as the McClintock Slave Riot, it started after free blacks made a rush for a woman and a child who had just been released by the court into the custody of James Kennedy and another slave owner named Howard Hollingsworth. The blacks were able to rescue the two fugitives and carry them across Hanover Street. They were pursued by Kennedy, who tripped and fell and was assaulted by the crowd. Present at the courthouse that day was a Dickinson College professor named John McClintock who had earlier advised the court of a new state law banning any county official from having any part in the recovery of fugitive slaves.

McClintock had a reputation for being an outspoken critic of slavery. He saw its abolition as coming through religious reform in the attitudes toward it. To McClintock, slavery had no basis in scripture and was incompatible with Christianity. This stance made him a target of community anger, and he was arrested on suspicion of instigating the riot. Witnesses claimed that McClintock cheered the blacks on and assured them that he would accept any consequences. He was brought to trial in late August 1847 and cleared of charges of simple riot, assault and breach of peace. Less than two months later, Daniel Kaufman was involved in the escape of the thirteen fugitive slaves. That incident formed the basis of the lawsuit that ended his part in the Underground Railroad.

In the court trials that followed, free black George Cole testified that he met the runaways in Chambersburg and took them away as a friend to prevent them from being sold. He transported them first to Shippensburg before arriving at the Kaufman farm on October 9, 1847. Cole hid the fugitives in the barn and went to the farmhouse to ask for Kaufman. On seeing the slaves, Kaufman asked Cole repeatedly to take them away, but Cole persisted and eventually Kaufman agreed to do all he could to help the fugitives make their escape. Meanwhile, the runaways were being hunted down by John Stake, a cousin of the Oliver family who owned the slaves.

In February 1846, Shadrach Oliver of Arkansas died, and his estate was divided up between his widow and children. In May 1847, the widow moved to Williamsport, Maryland, taking along her children and their slaves. Five months later, the slaves escaped, and Stake was able to track their movements to Chambersburg and then to the Kaufman farm, where he confronted Daniel's wife, who denied any knowledge of runaway slaves on their property. "I told her it was useless to deny it," Stake told jurors. "I had it from neighbors they had been there." At that point, she told Stake that her husband was away to fetch a load of wood and was only expected to return that evening. "I told her I intended to bring a suit against Kaufman for harboring and aiding those colored persons," Stake testified. Hearing that, she threatened a countersuit that never materialized.

Stake followed through on behalf of the Oliver family and pursued damages equal to the value of the escaped slaves. The county court trial resulted in a jury verdict in favor of the family, and Kaufman was fined $2,000, or about $51,000 in today's money. He then appealed the case to the Pennsylvania Supreme Court, which issued a ruling in June 1849. In it, the state court reversed the jury verdict on the grounds that Kaufman's alleged involvement with the escape was a violation of the Fugitive Slave Law and should be tried in federal court. Judge Richard Coulter delivered the following opinion from the bench: "The true question in this case is whether in Pennsylvania a citizen who gives a cup of water and a morsel of bread to famishing women and children and permits them to rest a few hours in his barn does by that offer of mercy and compassion break the law and make himself liable for their price in the mart where men, women and children are bought and sold."

This mansion at the corner of Front and Third Streets in Boiling Springs was once the home of Daniel Kaufman, founder of the village. *Photo by Joseph David Cress.*

In 1849, the Oliver family filed suit in federal court against Kaufman, his brother-in-law Stephen Weakley and Philip Brechbill, another man believed to have been involved in the Underground Railroad. On October 31, 1850, the *American Volunteer* reported that the jury could not decide on a verdict after being out all night. The panel was deadlocked with ten jurors in favor of the family and two against. The judge dismissed them, and another jury heard the case in 1852. The *American Democrat* reported that, on November 4, jurors ruled against Kaufman for $2,800 in damages and another $1,200 in costs. The other men were cleared of any involvement. Still, it wasn't an easy decision. The jury was out from Thursday morning to Saturday evening deliberating the case.

While they won, the slaveholders were not satisfied by the outcome. They wanted a larger sum of money from a responsible party. A verdict against Weakley was their objective, and their request for a new trial was soon granted. On the advice of Thaddeus Stevens and other prominent attorneys, Weakley came forward and offered to pay the entire judgment against Kaufman with interest and costs. "I put an end to that tormenting and oppressive lawsuit," Weakley would later write. "This was the best settlement that could be made to avoid the expense of another trial. I yielded up the money in the same principle I would to a highwayman."

The bill came out to $4,191—of which Weakley paid about $2,291 out of his pocket. The rest was paid with contributions made by an abolition society in Philadelphia. Even with the help, Weakley was left in dire financial straits. "I have borrowed in every conceivable way," he wrote. "My farm contained ninety acres, but under all these liabilities, I don't see how I could hold it with any prospect of getting out of debt." Meanwhile, it is said Kaufman became such a bitter enemy of the South that when Confederate forces invaded Cumberland County in June 1863, Kaufman rode his horse from Boiling Springs to the mountain overlooking the Holly Gap and took potshots at passing Rebel soldiers.

Beyond his involvement with the Underground Railroad, Kaufman was the founder of Boiling Springs. In 1849, he laid out the village on forty-seven acres of farmland purchased from his father, Abraham. He continued to sell lots from 1846 until his death in 1902. In 1853, Kaufman played a part in establishing the first public schools in the village. Known to local residents as "Uncle Dan," he lived at the farmhouse until around 1880 when he moved into a mansion at the corner of Front and Third Streets that still stands today. When he died on July 26, 1902, Kaufman was the oldest resident

This drawing of Boiling Springs was published in the 1879 book *History of Cumberland County* by Reverend Conway Wing. *Courtesy of CCHS.*

of Boiling Springs and was believed to be the last surviving member of the Underground Railroad network in Cumberland County. He is buried in the Mount Zion Cemetery near Churchtown.

There were two other court cases involving fugitive slaves heard at the Cumberland County courthouse. One involved the 1850 kidnapping of a black man born into freedom after his pregnant mother had fled slavery from Maryland. The other involved the 1859 abduction of an entire black family by slave catcher Emanuel Myers. Both cases are described in the next chapter.

1859: Kidnapped the Kidnapper

Sheriff Robert McCartney once used trickery to force a kidnapper to cross the line. He had a warrant from Cumberland County to arrest Emanuel Myers on charges the reputed slave catcher had abducted a black family from their home in Dickinson Township outside Carlisle on June 10, 1859. Trouble was Myers lived ten to twelve feet over the border in Maryland, where McCartney had no jurisdiction. This problem was solved by a bogus letter and a cooperative stagecoach driver.

The *American Volunteer* reported that McCartney had the man drive past Myers's home en route to Pennsylvania. As the vehicle went by, the driver held out a paper and shouted "Here Myers…Here's a letter for you!" Thinking it legitimate, Myers took off after the stagecoach, which continued on its way. All the while, the driver pretended to bring the horses to a stop but kept the animals moving at a fast trot until the vehicle went over the border into Pennsylvania. It was there in Adams County where the trap was sprung.

Unknown to Myers, McCartney was in the stagecoach hidden behind the drawn curtains. When it came to a halt, the sheriff slipped out on the side opposite Myers just as the driver was about to hand over the letter. McCartney circled around, grabbed his suspect by the collar and demanded his surrender, but Myers resisted, and for several minutes, the men were locked in a desperate struggle. At one point, Myers had the sheriff by the throat until McCartney wrestled the kidnapper to the ground. Drawing his pistol, McCartney threatened to shoot Myers if he did not surrender. At that moment, a Southern gentleman rushed to the scene to assist the sheriff in an arrest that set in motion a criminal trial that challenged the legality of fugitive slave laws.

In his book *History of Cumberland County*, Conway Wing explained how this incident caused excitement throughout Maryland and farther south. "The arrest was not only an outrage on one of her citizens, but a gross indignity to the state of Maryland. The newspapers united in denunciation of Northern aggression and called on authorities to vindicate the honor and dignity of a sovereign commonwealth." Local historian D.W. Thompson wrote how McCartney pursued Myers with "more zeal than legality" and "had no authority to make an arrest outside (Cumberland) County. He had, in fact, kidnapped the kidnapper."

The *Carlisle American* on June 22, 1859, praised the enterprising sheriff for making two arrests in short order in an abduction case that angered Cumberland County residents. "Robert McCartney…evinces a sagacity that would be a credit to the far-famed Bow Street runners of London," the newspaper reported. This case involved a mulatto named John Butler; his wife, Emaline; and their daughter, Elizabeth. The family lived near Spruce Run and was described by neighbors as good, hardworking people. The parents had jobs while the child attended school.

Early press accounts report the family was forcibly removed from their home sometime between nine and ten o'clock the evening of June 10, 1859. Back then, newspapers were not shy about mixing facts with commentary in a news story. "It is right that the people of Dickinson show indignation at the outrage…perpetrated in their midst," the *American Volunteer* reported. "We sincerely hope the vile scoundrels…guilty of this meanest of crimes will be arrested and severely punished."

The *Carlisle American* called it one of the most outrageous cases of kidnapping ever done in Cumberland County. "The secrecy with which the affair was conducted leaves little room to doubt…the parties were well acquainted with …the neighborhood and their nefarious business," the newspaper reported. The article mentioned how the abduction was made in a "thickly settled spot" populated by four to five white families "within a stone's throw" and "not the slightest alarm was raised." The crime was only discovered early the next morning when the house was found deserted.

John Morrison of Dickinson Township testified during the November 15, 1859 trial that Butler had worked for him on Friday, June 10 before leaving for home around sundown. The next morning between 12:00 and 2:00 a.m., three or four individuals came to Morrison's home and woke him up. The witness did not elaborate on why, who they were or what was said, only that

This photograph of the tollgate at Mount Holly Springs was taken from a postcard by Clyde A. Laughlin circa 1907. *Courtesy of CCHS.*

just before sunrise on June 11, he rode over to the Butler home about three-quarters of a mile away.

"I found the house open, went in and found no person there," Morrison told jurors. "The hat, coat and boots he [Butler] had worn the day before was lying here and there around the room." Morrison also saw clothing belonging to the wife and child scattered about the floor along with a snuffbox, "a likeness" and several trinkets. He said the wife was between thirty and thirty-three years old, while her daughter was between seven and nine years old. Morrison then went to a nearby stable, where he saw evidence that a carriage had turned around. He followed the tracks down Pine Road to the turnpike. His eyewitness account corresponded with a June 15 report by the *Carlisle American* that a carriage had forced its way through the Mount Holly Springs tollgate the same evening as the abduction.

Philip Clepper was the gatekeeper on duty on Friday, June 10, 1859. He testified at the trial that a carriage came through that day around 3:00 or 4:00 p.m. That evening between 11:00 p.m. and 12:00 a.m., Clepper heard a man call out to him to take the toll as a carriage approached the gate. "I jumped up, hoisted the window and saw the top of the carriage going through…as fast as the horses would run," Clepper told the jury. "When Myers was brought back by McCartney, he asked [me] if I found twenty-five cents upon my window sash. I told him I did, but could not tell whose money it was. He [Myers] said I am the one who left it there."

Early in the investigation, suspicion fell on a German immigrant and gunsmith named Valentine Gass—a man described by the *American Volunteer* as "a hang dog looking rascal." Gass allegedly pointed out the Butler home to the kidnappers on the promise of receiving ten dollars for his trouble. It appeared that leads generated from the arrest of Gass led to the warrant being issued on Myers, whom the *Carlisle American* dubbed "the principal agent in this black and diabolical transaction."

That same newspaper sent a staff member to visit the prisoners at the county jail on the corner of North Bedford and East High streets in Carlisle. In its June 22 story, the *Carlisle American* described Gass as an ordinary-looking man "scared at the same time not exactly understanding his situation." As for Myers, he had a face that expressed firmness and resolve but little intelligence:

> [A] *few minutes conversation with him is sufficient to convince one...he is but a tool, an unprincipled one if you please, of the persons who really owned the negroes. He seems to care little for the fix he has gotten him*[self] *into and expresses his perfect willingness to go to the penitentiary if he has broken the law of which he seems to be entirely ignorant. He says...there were some four to five others engaged in the affair who managed the greater part of the business but as to their names...or as to giving any clue to them he keeps a closed mouth and when questioned as to the matter either laughs or else says nothing.*
>
> *We do most sincerely hope...the balance of the party may be apprehended and brought to justice and then the real leaders of this affair who have worked on this man's ignorance may be made to suffer at least equally with him.*

W.B. Mullin testified at trial that he had a conversation with Gass during which the defendant identified Myers as one of the kidnappers. It was reported that Myers also had a pistol repaired by Gass the night of the abduction. Fellow witness Richard Woods talked to Gass the Monday or Tuesday after the kidnapping. During their talk, Gass mentioned how Myers was among the men who stopped by his home to get their pistols repaired that night. While there, they asked about the road to Bendersville and offered to pay him ten dollars for information leading to the Butler family home, but they never followed through on their promise of money.

This circa 1900 photograph of the old Cumberland County jail was taken by local photographer A.A. Line. *Courtesy of CCHS.*

A third witness, Levi Stough, had a talk with Gass at the jail during which the suspect said he was standing by a roadside post when the conspirators drove up in a carriage and asked for directions to Bendersville. All three men had similar versions of the same story told to them by Gass. In it, the defendant snuck after the men in the carriage and followed them to a stable near the Butler home. There, Gass hid in the bushes and observed the kidnappers as they got out of the carriage armed with knives and pistols. In the end, the jury found Gass not guilty of criminal charges. Two other men—Henry Keefauver and tavern keeper Snyder Rupley—were also arrested in connection with the kidnapping but proved an alibi and were acquitted of charges by the jury.

Tobias Sites, a witness for the defense, testified that he was building a house and that Keefauver was doing some plastering for him around the same time the family was being abducted. As for Rupley, W. Wyer told jurors the tavern keeper was standing by the barroom door when the kidnappers left to commit the crime. Rupley did not get into the carriage with the strangers. This witness was at the tavern from sundown to about 11:00 p.m.

It was reported how attorneys for Myers never seriously challenged the fact that the family had been kidnapped. Instead, the key question for the jury was whether Emaline and Elizabeth were free blacks or fugitive slaves. While there was evidence proving that John Butler was a runaway slave, there was debate over the status of the mother and daughter in the context of the last will and testament of their late mistress Elizabeth Warfield.

Defense called Dennis Maynard, who testified that on June 11, 1859, he saw Myers with the Butler family in Johnsville, Maryland. This witness told jurors he knew John Butler by a different name, "Reason," and described the father as a raw, bony man with a beard and a mustache. While he knew Emaline for fifteen years, Maynard had only known the man and child since 1856. When he first met Emaline, she was property of Surat De Warfield until his death in 1851 or 1852. Emaline and her daughter then became the property of Elizabeth Warfield.

The prosecution argued that when Elizabeth Warfield died in 1854, her will freed the mother and daughter and that four years had gone by where the executor of her estate exercised no control over the former slaves. However, the defense argued that the release of the slaves was a fraud committed by Warfield to avoid paying debt owed to creditors. Attorneys for Myers tried to convince jurors that the estate was insolvent and that their client and the executor had a right to capture and sell the slaves to earn the money they needed to settle the estate.

In its coverage, the *American Volunteer* reported that the defense claim was thought by some to have been a ruse cooked up only to get the extra money the slaves would have brought in. It was believed the estate had plenty of resources with which to pay off the debt. By contrast, the status of John Butler was clear. Maynard testified that, in 1856, the slave he called "Reason" was sold by John Warfield, the estate executor, to Theodore Hoffman. Later, Reason ran away with his family to Pennsylvania sometime in May or June 1858 only to settle in Dickinson Township. In the end, the court settled on a compromise resolution where Myers was found guilty of kidnapping, but the prosecution did not press for a sentence in exchange for the family being allowed to return to Cumberland County.

Myers's was not the only kidnapping case involving fugitive slaves heard before a Cumberland County jury. On April 10, 1850, a trial was held for Martin Auld accused in the abduction of eighteen-year-old Alexander Burns, a free black who was born in Pennsylvania but sold into slavery in

This illustration is from the 1872 book *The Underground Railroad* by William Still. *Courtesy of CCHS.*

Baltimore. In 1831, a female slave named Betsy escaped into Pennsylvania from the property of a Dr. Ridgely of Maryland. Six months after her arrival in the Keystone State, Betsy gave birth to Alexander. Somehow, Auld found out that mother and child were living in the Carlisle area, so he wrote a letter to Ridgely, who dispatched his two sons to reclaim the lost property.

The sons hired Auld and an innkeeper named Pile to help them capture the boy. There was no further mention in sources of what happened to Betsy, only that she married and had several more children after she gave birth to Alexander. Instead of capturing her, the conspirators hatched a plot where Pile would hire Alexander to care for the horses of Ridgely's sons. This seemed a feasible plan. After all, Pile had hired the boy before for the same kind of work.

At first, the men enticed Alexander to drink brandy laced with laudanum, an extract of opium, but the drug did not have the desired effect. The kidnappers then convinced the boy to ride along with them in a carriage in order to point out the road they wished to take. The boy got suspicious after the carriage passed the point where they were supposed to let him off. When Alexander tried to make a noise, Auld stuffed a handkerchief in his mouth as they carried him off to Baltimore.

The *Carlisle American* condemned the act, stating, "The conduct of the parties implicated in the transaction has certainly all…the elements of a crime and none of the outward marks of a claim of property." In particular, the newspaper mentioned how Auld and company spent days "maturing their plans…to lure the victim into helplessness" and picked "the dead hour of the night" to commit the crime.

Ultimately, the jury found Auld guilty of kidnapping on the grounds that, since Alexander was born in the free state of Pennsylvania, he could not be considered a fugitive slave. As a result, a state law punishing those who forcibly remove free blacks applied. Alexander was eventually released from slavery. While this case was resolved, the overriding issue of slavery in America was not. The *Herald* summed up the dilemma as follows: "The questions of law that arise in this case present one of the points of a subject which agitates the whole country and occupies the minds of our greatest men."

1861: Outburst of Patriotism

It began when a lone rider arrived in Carlisle with a rude awakening just before 1:00 a.m. on April 24, 1861. He had news that five thousand Rebel soldiers were on the march, bent on the destruction of the barracks just outside of town. The Confederate force was led by former officers of the U.S. Army who knew the post was relatively defenseless. It was believed the enemy had already set fire to Hanover in York County and was heading north for the Holly Gap.

Looking back, the *Carlisle Herald* recalled a rumor that was hard to believe but alarming enough to cause great excitement. "Bells were rung...Drums beat to arms and in a short time, the volunteer companies were forming on the Square," the newspaper reported. "The streets were crowded with our citizens while women and children were preparing to move at short notice." Local historian Conway Wing described how men "hurried through the streets in search of weapons" and "gazed as if for the last time upon their helpless wives and children. Mothers clasped their infants to their bosoms that they might die together."

"Before the people had learned anything of modern civil war, the most improbable reports of cruelty and devastation were readily credited," Wing explained the mindset of the time. "It was stated the enemy was advancing with fire and sword spreading death, ruin and desolation...Soon the greatest consternation prevailed. The night was full of horror, and vivid imaginations already descried the reflection of the flames of burning buildings on the distant horizon and snuffed the smoke in the midnight air."

By 3:00 a.m., the alarm had subsided when a second messenger came into town. He confirmed the story of the first rider and said he was sent to Carlisle to procure ammunition. The *Herald* reported how both men were highly respected and known by many local residents. The newspaper withheld their names. The *American Volunteer*, a rival publication, had this to say on what happened next: "The excitement was greater than ever. A number of children were taken from their beds and hurried out of town. The troops were again put in motion. Old guns of every description were brought out and an early attack upon our town was expected by most of our people. The infantry company, well armed, marched to Papertown in double quick time for the purpose of intercepting the marauders." Papertown was the name local residents had for Mount Holly Springs—a small town about six miles to the south and known for its high-quality paper mills.

This Carlisle contingent was under the command of Captain Robert McCartney and included in its ranks Jacob Ritner, son of the former governor Joseph Ritner. "The gentleman rode into town at break of day armed with a…musket and a pocketful of buckshot," Wing wrote. Within hours, Mount Holly Springs was crowded with militia who occupied the mountain pass in anticipation of the arrival of an enemy that never came. "The first rays of the morning sun…dispelled both the mists on the mountain and the fear of invasion," Wing described the scene.

The *Evening Sentinel* recalled "the bloodless battle of Mt. Holly Gap" in a July 1, 1916 story about the town celebrating its 100th anniversary. "Upon reaching the town, they took fortified positions in the Gap, ready to sweep like a besom (broom) of destruction upon the foe. To achieve this mighty victory, they came with flintlock muskets, many minus locks, and others armed with knives for closer conflict in the mountain passes. The company had come prepared to die in the last ditch." The article mentioned how local farmers joined in "to show the metal of their pasture," presumably with farm implements as weapons.

In his *History of Cumberland County*, Wing saluted the brave defenders of Mount Holly Springs: "Though no foe appeared…Mother Cumberland might be proud of this outburst of patriotism and feel reassured that whatever circumstances shall require it her sons shall arise as one man for defense." "Mother Cumberland" was a reference to a bygone era when Cumberland County was much larger and extended from the Susquehanna River west to just beyond Pittsburgh. By 1861, this vast territory had split into fragments. Forty-eight of the sixty-seven counties in Pennsylvania can trace something of their territorial roots back to Cumberland County.

This stereograph by John Choate depicts the Mount Holly Gap circa 1876 to 1880. *Courtesy of CCHS.*

Carlisle newspapers had conflicting reports on the source of this false rumor. The *Herald* said the rumor started when men pushing a handcart from Hanover to Gettysburg pulled a prank on some passing travelers asking them for news. The men told them that Rebels were within three miles of Hanover and had threatened to burn down the town. The *American Volunteer* traced the rumor to a large group of men moving after dark. It was later determined that these were slaves escaping their masters in Maryland.

While no battle took place, the false alarm did result in a civilian death. Nineteen-year-old William Beetem and his uncle J.U. Wunderlich were traveling by buggy along the Hanover turnpike when they encountered the infantry company marching back to Carlisle. Seeing how tired the soldiers were, they offered to carry some muskets. As it was being loaded onto the buggy, a gun

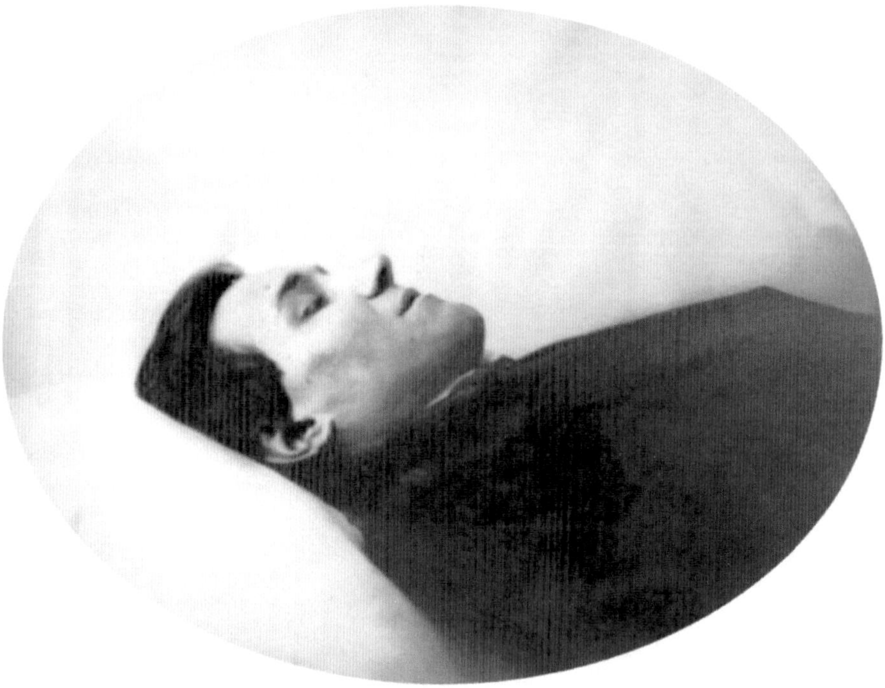

This postmortem cased tintype shows William Beetem lying in state shortly after his accidental shooting in April 1861. *Courtesy of CCHS.*

accidentally discharged. The bullet passed through Beetem's heart, killing him instantly. "This sad incident cast a gloom over our town and has overwhelmed the mother of the boy with grief," the *Herald* reported. "The body of the deceased arrived at this mother's residence an hour or so after the accident." Eventually, communications were open with York where nothing was known of a rebel force marching through Pennsylvania. Carlisle residents were in a state of alarm until long after daybreak, the *Volunteer* reported. "No enemy appearing, the excitement...quieted down. Most citizens then partook of a hearty breakfast."

Other soldiers deployed from Carlisle destroyed the federal arsenal at Harpers Ferry. The election of President Abraham Lincoln in November 1860 prompted South Carolina to secede from the Union on December 20. Ten other Southern states would follow suit. On January 10, 1861, the U.S. Army ordered a company of mounted riflemen under Lieutenant Roger Jones to march from Carlisle Barracks and board a train to Baltimore. Later, this force of forty-three men was dispatched to Harpers Ferry to guard the arsenal. On April 12, 1861, Fort Sumter was fired on by secessionist forces triggering the start of the American

Civil War. A week later, Jones received word that a greatly superior enemy force under General Kenton Harper was on its way to capture the installation.

"From an early day…it became evident a defense of the valuable interests at Harpers Ferry would be impractical unless large reinforcements were sent there," Rogers would later report. "As there was every reason for believing this would not be done, I early on became convinced there was but one course of action to pursue to destroy what could not be defended. Trains of gunpowder were laid through the buildings to be fired. In the shops, men with Southern sympathies managed to wet the powder in many places, rendering it harmless."

Jones explained that since he was operating entirely on his own judgment, he was determined not to act prematurely, but only when danger was imminent. "As this evening advanced, nearer and nearer came the troops…and finally, shortly after nine o'clock, they had advanced to less than a mile of the armory. The torch was applied. Before I could withdraw my men from the village, the two arsenal buildings containing about twenty thousand…rifles and muskets were ablaze. Very few of those arms were saved from the constantly reoccurring explosions of powder."

The *American Democrat* of Carlisle reported that Jones had War Department orders to destroy "all munitions of war, the armory, the arsenal and all its buildings." The newspaper stated about 2,500 soldiers had been ordered by

This illustration from *Harper's Weekly* shows the April 18, 1861 burning of the U.S. arsenal at Harpers Ferry. *Courtesy of Library of Congress.*

Virginia governor John Letcher to take the installation. "He (Jones) immediately placed piles of powder and straw in all the buildings and waited patiently for the approach of the enemy. The picket guard having given the alarm, the garrison set fire to the outhouses and the carpenter shop. The fuses beginning to burn, he commenced his retreat."

At that point, Harpers Ferry residents called themselves to arms and followed the Union troops as they rushed across a bridge over the Potomac River. Jones told the newspaper that other civilians ran to the arsenal, where he believed a number had died in the explosions. The burning buildings could be seen for miles. Under cover of darkness, this Carlisle detachment marched all night and the next day by way of Hagerstown and Chambersburg to return to Carlisle Barracks.

Missing from the detachment were four soldiers Jones had posted as sentries at Harpers Ferry to make sure the fire did not go out. These men were captured and offered rank as noncommissioned officers in the Confederate army. They refused to turn traitor, and on the night of April 20, 1861, two escaped over the bridge while a third swam the river and canal. The three fugitives arrived in Carlisle just days later to report that six thousand to seven thousand Virginians were at Harpers Ferry with five thousand more expected from Richmond. The *American Volunteer* predicted an invasion of Maryland was imminent. The final sentry, Private Moran, also managed to escape back to Carlisle Barracks, arriving there on May 2, 1861.

Just over two years later, Cumberland County was in the path of a real invasion by the Army of Northern Virginia. Confederate general Robert E. Lee launched a campaign to seize Harrisburg, a Northern capital and vital transportation hub, but ended up losing decisively at the Battle of Gettysburg. In its 1916 tribute to Mount Holly's centennial, the *Evening Sentinel* estimated that about forty thousand Union and Confederate soldiers had passed through the town from late June to early July 1863. While in Mount Holly, Southern troops under Lieutenant General Richard Ewell confiscated over $4,000 worth of high-quality stock from the Kempton & Mullin paper company.

The Rebels gave the firm a receipt, enjoining them not to allow a single ream of paper to be removed from the mill without an order from Ewell, the *Philadelphia Public Ledger* reported. Other mills were treated in a like manner with receipts being given for the stock taken and injunctions laid on the proprietors to give no paper to anyone. The Rebels told the paper manufacturers that the stock they contributed to the Confederate government was the most desirable article yet captured. It was greatly needed in the departments of Richmond and would be welcomed with more satisfaction by President Jefferson Davis than a dozen captured Union standards.

1863: Exclusively Gentlemen

Always the gentleman, the Confederate cavalryman removed his cap in a show of respect before starting his interrogation with a pleasant, "Good morning ladies." Reverend John Miller remembered the day when, as local tradition has it, the Army of Northern Virginia achieved its farthest reach into Northern territory during the Gettysburg campaign. There was no exchange of gunfire or desperate heroics, just a band of Rebel scouts with a few questions and a group of children with some answers.

"Did you ever see any Rebels before?" the enemy soldier asked. "Yes, we saw one of your men go by a prisoner a few days ago," replied Sarah, John's sister. "Oh, that was only a straggler," the cavalryman responded. "Now look upon us. We are real genuine Rebels, and don't be afraid of us. We will do you no harm." "We are never afraid of gentlemen," said Barbara, another sister. One can imagine the trooper sitting proud in the saddle as he added emphasis to his next words. "We are gentlemen; the Rebel army is composed *exclusively* of gentlemen."

There were many in the Cumberland Valley who would disagree that late June and early July 1863. As the Confederate soldiers advanced, they confiscated preserved meat, canned goods, medical supplies, grain, horses and cattle from the civilian population. Many local residents tried to hide their livestock beyond North Mountain in Perry County, while others fled east across the Susquehanna River to Harrisburg as refugees.

But Harrisburg was hardly safe. Indeed, this key transportation hub for the North was the real target of the 1863 invasion. Taking it would have given

This portrait of Reverend John Miller is from the A.A. Line Collection. *Courtesy of CCHS.*

the Rebels much-needed logistical support. Capturing a Northern capital could also have persuaded France and England to recognize the South as an independent nation and provide diplomatic and financial support. Further, it was believed a victory on Union soil could alter the political dynamics of the war-weary North and convince voters in upcoming elections to select candidates more willing to negotiate peace. None of that happened because the main battle was fought at Gettysburg.

Only nine years old at the time, John Miller would recall decades later how fear and confusion spread throughout the Cumberland Valley at the approach of the Confederate army. On June 27, 1863, his father, Joseph, returned from Carlisle to report how Rebel soldiers marched down what is now West High Street toward the square. Back then, the Miller family lived on the John Kutz farm, located at the foot of Sterretts Gap about one mile north of Carlisle Springs in Middlesex Township.

On June 28, John Miller was enjoying a beautiful Sunday morning outside with his three sisters, a brother and a cousin. The children were eating fruit from a cherry tree that grew along the road. They were startled by the sudden appearance of a Union soldier on horseback galloping rapidly toward Carlisle Springs. One of the sisters remarked that the soldier was taking a risk and was perhaps unaware that the Rebels had occupied Carlisle. "Neither did we know that a detachment of about twenty Rebel cavalrymen had half an hour previously arrived at Carlisle Springs and at that very time were galloping down the road towards our home," Miller recalled.

The children saw the Union horseman return up the slope a short time later after being warned to turn back by George Jacobs, a neighbor of the Miller family. The soldier stopped to talk to the children. "What kind of a man is that up on the hill? He tells me the Rebels are coming. Is he reliable?" The children quickly reassured the man that Jacobs can be trusted. Just then Confederate cavalrymen were seen dashing over the crest of the hill toward their location. On seeing that, the Union soldier applied the spurs to his horse and galloped away north toward Sterretts Gap.

This pass over North Mountain was blocked during the invasion by log barriers hurriedly constructed by men from Marysville. As commander of the newly formed Department of the Susquehanna, Major General Darius Couch was responsible for the Union defenses around Harrisburg. He quickly realized the Confederates could funnel troops through the mountain passes and down the valleys north of the mountain range to the Marysville-Duncannon area and then cross the river to take Harrisburg from the north. Couch ordered the passes fortified with roadblocks and rifle pits manned by armed civilians from Perry County and commanded by former officers.

Just as the Union soldier disappeared from view, about half the Confederate cavalrymen, with pistols in hand, stopped opposite to where the children were standing. What followed was that brief exchange of comments about soldiers being gentlemen before a few more questions were asked by the enemy. "What was the import of that Yank's interview with you a few moments ago?" The children replied that the soldier had asked whether the man on the hill was reliable and could his warning be believed.

With that, the Rebel spokesman asked the children if it would be prudent for him to advance any farther north toward Sterretts Gap. They told him it would not be advisable. So the Southern gentlemen said goodbye to the children, wheeled their horses around and galloped south several hundred yards to where the other half of the detachment waited. John Miller noticed how these other troopers had their handkerchiefs out frantically trying to signal their comrades to turn back.

Confederates had reason to be nervous beyond the word of some children. Earlier, they had entered Carlisle Springs, where a former Carlisle businessman named Nathan Woods managed a summer resort. "During their visit, they emphatically declared to Woods, 'You are no longer under the administration of Abe Lincoln, but under that of Jefferson Davis,'" Miller recalled the story. Woods suggested that the Rebels stay away from Sterretts Gap, claiming sources told him that there were fifty thousand Union soldiers guarding the mountain pass. These troops were not only well

This state marker one mile north of Carlisle Springs along Route 34 designates the northernmost point reached by any element of the Confederate army during the Gettysburg campaign. *Photo by Joseph David Cress.*

entrenched but also supplied with artillery that could command the whole of the Cumberland Valley from Chambersburg to Harrisburg. This, of course, was an exaggeration of what actually waited for them.

On September 19, 1927, the *Evening Sentinel* in Carlisle reported the details of a recent visit to Sterretts Gap made by Lieutenant M.H. McCall, a Civil War veteran of the Union army. McCall explained how he led a company of volunteers to the top of North Mountain to guard this pass from an anticipated invasion of Confederate forces. McCall mentioned the need to prevent the Rebels from confiscating the large herds of horses and cattle driven to shelter on the Perry County side of North Mountain.

McCall remembered how his men constructed stone breastworks—of which he found no trace. Aside from militia units, there were hundreds of old men, young boys and women stationed at vantage points along the ridge to watch for the Confederate approach, McCall said. But according to local tradition, the Army of Northern Virginia only got as far as where the Miller family placed a marker in October 1929 near Carlisle Springs. Reverend John Miller was the only eyewitness present who could testify to the exchange of words between the Confederate cavalrymen and his relatives on June 28,

1863. Miller told the story of the account during the dedication ceremony for the marker. He concluded his comments with the following words, as quoted by the *Sentinel*:

> *The imposition of Providence has turned back the invading host. Our enemies, before leaving our beautiful valley, as a reminder of their visit, shelled Carlisle, burned the old barracks and moved to their Waterloo at Gettysburg. In carrying out our program, we do not so for the purpose of perpetuating war or fostering the spirit of militarism. We recognize war as demoralizing, unchristian and deplorable. There have been occasions in which war became a painful necessity. I believe the sword should never be resorted to until all other measures of peace have failed.*

1863: Saber Blade Dazzle

When North and South collided, the crash was akin to falling timber. The impact was so violent that horses tumbled end over end, crushing their riders beneath them. "The clashing of sabers, the firing of pistols, the demands for surrender…filled the air," recalled Captain William Miller, a Newville-area native. He knew that a critical moment had arrived on that third day of the Battle of Gettysburg. Miller realized his next move would be in direct violation of orders to hold ground and stay concealed. Yet the situation was grim and demanded quick action. What followed would earn Miller the distinction of being the first and perhaps only soldier in U.S. Army history to earn the Medal of Honor for defying the commands of his superior officer.

The Third Pennsylvania Volunteer Cavalry Regiment was among the units guarding the extreme right flank of the Union Army of the Potomac on July 3, 1863. In command of Company H, Miller was in charge of eighty troopers assigned to occupy Lott's Woods along Low Dutch Road north of Hanover Road and just over two miles southeast of Gettysburg. Miller recalled how his men were worn out and "our ranks very much depleted" following two days of skirmishes and running fights against Confederate cavalry under Major General J.E.B. Stuart. On that morning of July 3, Miller and his men were recovering from a brush with enemy infantry the night before.

Stuart and his four brigades had arrived in Gettysburg on the afternoon of July 2. The next morning, his force of about 6,300 men were deployed in woods on Cress Ridge, north of where Union generals David Gregg and George Custer had positioned about 4,500 cavalrymen along Hanover Road. The plan that day was for Stuart to overrun the Union right flank and cut through the rear of the lines before joining up with infantry under Major General George Pickett, who had orders to charge across the open field and into the Union center on Cemetery Ridge.

Around noon, Confederate horse artillery fired on Union positions, and Stuart ordered dismounted cavalry forward to occupy a barn on the Rummel farm. Two hours later, Union colonel John McIntosh learned of Stuart's tactic and ordered dismounted cavalry from the First New Jersey Regiment forward to capture the barn. Heavy fighting ensued. Around this time, McIntosh ordered part of the Third Pennsylvania, including Company H, to occupy the right flank near the Lott Farm. The rest of the regiment was sent to help the New Jersey men who were further reinforced by the Fifth Michigan Cavalry Regiment.

When the Fifth Michigan was driven back, Custer ordered the Seventh Michigan Cavalry Regiment to mount up and charge the Confederates, but the Seventh was also repulsed. The whole time, Miller maintained his position in Lott's Woods. He would later describe the scene. "The troopers in my command were resting—either lying on the ground or using trees as a back rest. Each…had the reins of the horse in his hands, ready to mount without delay. I was standing on the edge of the woods surveying the field with my field glasses and keeping watch in the direction…where I had been informed…Confederate cavalry was stationed. The sound of heavy firing…caused me to study more carefully the ground in front of the Confederate position." To the east, enemy artillery was firing into the Union center in preparation for Pickett's Charge.

Around 3:00 p.m., Stuart assembled about two thousand cavalrymen commanded by Wade Hampton and Fitzhugh Lee, both brigadier generals. Their mission was to make a final push to dislodge the Union cavalry. Miller described how these Confederate horsemen braved Union artillery as they moved across the field only to run headlong into the First Michigan Cavalry Regiment deployed to counter the move:

> *They marched with well-aligned fronts and steady reins. Their polished saber blades dazzled in the sun. All eyes were turned upon them. Shell and shrapnel met the advancing Confederates and tore through their ranks. Closing the gaps, on they came. As they drew nearer, canister was substituted for…shell and horse after horse staggered and fell. Still they came on. Our*

> *mounted skirmishers rallied and fell into line. The dismounted men fell back and a few of them reached their horses. The First Michigan drawn up in close columns of squadrons was ordered to charge. Custer, who was near, placed himself at the head, and off they dashed. As the two columns approached each other, the pace of each increased.*

What followed was the crashing sound that Miller compared to falling timber followed by fierce hand-to-hand combat. From their vantage point atop a knoll, Miller and his Adjutant Lieutenant William Brooke Rawle had an "elegant view of all that was going on," as the captain would later put it. "We soon discovered that Stuart was too heavy for Custer, and unless some diversion was made, all would be lost," Miller said. "I realized immediately…the Union lines would be crushed between Pickett in front and Stuart in the rear." Just to the right of Miller's position, D.M. Gilmore, a captain in Company D of the Third Pennsylvania, was awed by the sight of the Confederate cavalry advance and what it could mean for the Union cause:

> *Their erect bodies and deliberate movements indicated their determination to march through our thin lines and complete their purpose of creating havoc and panic in the rear of our army. Every man on our side realized that the critical moment was at hand. To turn back or to even check the advance of this apparently irresistible body seemed almost hopeless, but the effort had to be made and all prepared for the mighty conflict.*

For Miller, the moment of decision had arrived. "I took a chance. I ordered a charge through Stuart's command." But before he could issue the order, Miller needed some reassurance. He turned to Rawle and said, "I have been ordered to hold this position, but if you back me up in case I am court-martialed for disobedience, I will order a charge." Miller was never mentioned in the official War Department record of the Battle of Gettysburg. In late June 1897, an application for a Medal of Honor was submitted on behalf of this defiant soldier. Rawle was among the veterans who testified in an affidavit in support of the application. In it, he spoke of his response to Miller and what happened next:

> *I assured him…that I would stand by him through thick and thin. He then ordered me to rally the left wing of the squadron while he did the same on its right. When this was done, the squadron fired a volley into the Confederate column, which was within easy range. The men*

This circa 1862 photograph shows Captain William E. Miller in his Civil War uniform. *Courtesy of CCHS.*

were very impatient to begin their charge and the right wing, headed by Captain Miller, started off at a gallop. A stone and rail fence divided the line of the squadron front, running at right angles to it, and I had to make a slight detour to get around it for the left wing of the squadron. This and the fact that...the squadron was heading somewhat to the right oblique caused a gap of some thirty yards or so between the rear

> *portion of the squadron under Captain Miller and myself at the head of the left portion.*
>
> *Captain Miller with his men struck the left flank of the enemy's column pretty well towards its rear about two-thirds or three-fourths of the way down and as the impetus of the latter* [the Confederate column] *had stopped, his men had full headway on and he* [Miller] *drove well into the column and cut off its rear and forced it back into the direction from whence it came and the captain and some of his men got as far as the Rummel house.*

Meanwhile, the rear portion or left wing of the squadron did not succeed in forcing its way through the Confederate column, Rawle said. "Just as I and my men reached the flank of the enemy, many of the latter were getting to the rear and we were swept along with the current and scattered." The lieutenant narrowly escaped capture. Working their way through in "ones and twos," Rawle and his men managed to return to the Union line. The Medal of Honor application also included an eyewitness account of the charge by George Heagy, a sergeant in Company H. "After reaching Rummel's buildings, Captain Miller attempted to capture a battery on the rising ground close by, but did not succeed in rallying enough men to take charge of it," Heagy said. "I was with him up to the mouth of the guns. In the midst of the charge, my hat was knocked off with the blow of a saber…Had I not made a sudden parry, my head would have gone with it."

The battery Heagy was referring to was commanded by Captain James Breathed and was the same horse artillery that shelled Carlisle just two days before. The Confederate cavalry attack had temporarily silenced the guns. The Rebels did not want any casualties from friendly fire. Partway through his charge, Miller was shot in the right arm as he turned the right wing of his squadron north and then east. His troopers advanced through the enemy until they neared the lane of the Rummel farm where most were hemmed in and halted. At first, Miller thought that if he rode up the hill toward the battery, he could rally his men to take the guns, but the charge and subsequent fighting left only four men available to support such an assault. By that time, his charge had the desired effect, as the *Sentinel* newspaper described in its obituary on Miller that was published on December 10, 1919.

"So unexpected was it, and so impetuous, that it went right through the gray column, throwing it into confusion and cutting off, for a time, one-third of the strength of the supporting forces…The shock was so great that the Confederate column wavered." This sudden diversion by Miller helped Custer to rally his troops in front of the enemy advance and prompted other squadrons of the Third Pennsylvania to charge into the flanks of the Confederate cavalry. "In a short time the grey squadrons, broken and discomfited, were streaming back to their old position," the obituary reads. The attack repulsed, the Union right flank was secure and the center line held against Pickett's Charge. The North had won the Battle of Gettysburg.

There was no effort made to court-martial Captain Miller. Major General David Gregg lent his support of the Medal of Honor application by writing "the charge made by Captain Miller was a gallant one and aided materially in bringing success to our arms." Gregg went a step further and spoke directly with Secretary of War Russell Alger who, thirty-four years earlier, was the colonel in command of the Fifth Michigan Cavalry Regiment that fought in the same action to protect the Union right flank. Even though Gregg did not witness Miller's charge, he learned of it through conversations he had with Rawle and brigade and regimental commanders. The application was approved, and in July 1897, Alger presented Miller with the Medal of Honor.

Miller had a distinguished career as a soldier long before Gettysburg. He was born on February 5, 1836, in West Hill on the Newville Road in West Pennsboro Township. The oldest of six children of Andrew and Eleanor Umberger Miller, William took over from his invalid father and managed the family farm. Tending to the homestead left little time for anything more than a basic education. At age sixteen, Miller enlisted in a company of horse militia called the Big Spring Adamantine Guard. For the next nine years, he settled into a pattern of operating the farm and attending weekly cavalry drills. On October 23, 1856, William married Elizabeth Ann Hocker, his childhood sweetheart, and together they had daughters Caroline and Lizzie. Tragedy struck in 1859 when Elizabeth died of typhoid.

When the war started in April 1861, the Guard was among the first militia units to volunteer, but cavalrymen were excluded from the initial call for three-month enlistments. It was August 1861 before Guard members were allowed to enlist for three years under the designation of Company H of the Third Pennsylvania Volunteer Cavalry Regiment. Miller was commissioned a second lieutenant because of his long service with the militia. The regiment underwent rigid training at Camp Marcy, Virginia, during the winter of 1861–62. That March, Miller received a letter from his in-laws with news that his youngest daughter, Lizzie, had taken ill and died.

A month later, his regiment was deployed to Fort Monroe on the tip of the Virginia peninsula between the York and James Rivers. Union major general George B. McClellan had planned to move his army east to capture the Confederate capital of Richmond. In preparation for this assault, Miller was ordered to ride ahead into enemy territory and map out the roads that led to the James River. Several times, this assignment took Miller as deep as twenty miles behind the Confederate lines. This campaign to capture Richmond failed.

On September 16, 1862, Company H was assigned to the headquarters of Major General Joseph Hooker and helped to lead the Union I Corps across Antietam Creek in preparation for battle the next day. September 17 would become the single bloodiest day in American history. By the time it was over, the Battle of Antietam would claim nearly four thousand dead and about nineteen thousand wounded. Miller played a key role at a critical phase late in the afternoon as Confederate major general Thomas "Stonewall" Jackson made his final push toward the Union line. Jackson had ordered a brigade from his corps to charge a Union gun battery. Miller passed behind the

This photograph by A.A. Line shows Captain William E. Miller in the Hamilton Library with an exhibit he prepared for the 1901 sesquicentennial celebration of the founding of Cumberland County. Miller is considered to be the father of the Cumberland County Historical Society museum. *Courtesy of CCHS.*

battery and helped to save it from the superior enemy force. For his gallantry, he was promoted to captain ahead of all the first lieutenants in the regiment and was given command of Company H.

Less than two years later, on August 24, 1864, Captain Miller left the army after completing his enlistment. All told, he participated in thirty-seven engagements, including Brandy Station, the largest cavalry battle of the war. He returned to Cumberland County, where he later moved to Carlisle, remarried and operated a hardware store on North Hanover Street from 1868 to 1898. While in business, Miller became secretary of the Carlisle board of trade, devoting much of his time and energy toward the promotion of industry in town. He also served on the town board of health for about twelve years including four years as its president.

A well-known Democrat, Miller was active in politics. He was elected twice as chief burgess of Carlisle. At the urging of members of both political parties, Miller made a run for state office and was elected as the senator representing Cumberland and Adams Counties. He also served as chairman of the party's county committee and was selected to be a member of the party's central Pennsylvania committee. In 1912, Miller was appointed to the state commission preparing to commemorate the fiftieth anniversary of the Battle of Gettysburg. In May 1919, he suffered a stroke only to die about five months later at his home on North Hanover Street.

1888: Court of Last Resort

Michael Smyser testified that he became a believer after hearing the lyrics, "Don't you want to be a Christian while you're young?" He was in the upper room of the workshop of the "Wizard of Eberly's Mill" listening intently to the young boy singing through a tin box. The tonal quality was so distinctive, it was as though the child was standing right there beside him, but the boy was in the cellar two flights down. Partway through the demonstration, inventor Daniel Drawbaugh opened the door and shouted instructions to the youngster to count to five in a whisper. The boy obeyed, and his voice came out of the strange mechanism as clear as can be. It was 1872—more than three years before Alexander Graham Bell filed his patent. The legal dispute over who really invented the telephone would take Drawbaugh of Lower Allen Township all the way to the U.S. Supreme Court, where he lost his most important claim to fame and was hung up by history.

Smyser was among dozens of witnesses who, in 1886, testified before the U.S. Circuit Court of the Southern District of New York on behalf of the People's Telephone Company. Drawbaugh had sold the firm his rights to his talking machine for $5,000 in cash and an undisclosed amount of company stock. The American Bell Telephone Company promptly sued People's Telephone, claiming that it had violated Bell's 1876 patent. Numerous Cumberland County residents told the court that they saw various models of telephones in Drawbaugh's workshop going back as far as 1864. It is believed the tinkerer, known by neighbors as the Wizard, developed an acoustic telephone in 1866 that had a teacup as a transmitter and mustard

Reputed inventor of the telephone Daniel Drawbaugh sits in front of his workshop in Eberly's Mill with his grandson Roy Sheely. *Courtesy of CCHS.*

can as a receiver. Investors in Harrisburg showed no interest in Drawbaugh's invention, preferring instead to support upgrades to the telegraph. While there was testimony he had perfected a working model as early as 1874, Drawbaugh only applied for a patent in late July 1880. Money was an issue for him.

Drawbaugh once confided in Smyser that poverty was interfering with his ability to apply for a patent. "He couldn't work at the machine all the time because he had to do something else to sustain his family," this witness told the court. Nevertheless, Smyser testified how the device, on the day of the demonstration, used electricity supplied by a green coil to transmit the boy's voice from the cellar to the upper room. At one point in the visit, a confident Drawbaugh told Smyser that he could make a talking machine that could transmit voices from Pennsylvania to California. The Wizard clearly had a talent for invention going back to childhood.

Born on July 14, 1827, Drawbaugh was the fourth child of a blacksmith and descended from a long line of tinkerers, machinists and mechanics.

Historian Jerry Zeamer once told the story of how Drawbaugh received a flogging in school after his ingenuity got him into trouble. The boy had noticed how the loose-fitting door and window frames did little to protect the teacher and the students from drafts. So one night Drawbaugh constructed a miniature windmill out of tin to bring to school the next day. When the teacher wasn't looking, he set up the machine to catch the air current. It made such a whistling sound that it distracted the entire class, and Drawbaugh was punished after he first explained to classmates how the device operated. Growing up, he preferred tinkering in a workshop to attending school. It is said that by age twelve, he was fabricating parts for an electromagnetic clock, and by seventeen, he invented a rifle.

In his lifetime, Drawbaugh received about seventy patents for such devices as an automatic boiler feeder, a stave jointing machine, a steam injector, an automatic fire alarm, a coin sorter, a folding lunch box, a mowing machine and a paper bag folder. He designed a clock that ran off the Earth's electrical current and a pneumatic stone drill workers used in the construction of the Library of Congress. While he had ingenuity, Drawbaugh lacked marketing and business skills and never made more than $400 a year off his inventions. "He was no promoter…He was a creative genius," said Fern Hetrick, a distant relative. "He wasn't motivated by money and the material things of this life. He was able to use his head, heart and hands." That being said, for most of his eighty-four years, Drawbaugh was heavily in debt and once had to borrow $5 just to attend his father's funeral. Some believe his lack of savvy played a key role in the lawsuit that ended on March 19, 1888, when the U.S. Supreme Court decided four-to-three that Bell, not Drawbaugh, was the original inventor of the telephone. The landmark decision removed the last significant challenge to Bell's patent, clearing the way for him to develop a powerful monopoly. While one Supreme Court justice was absent due to illness, another excused himself from the case because he owned Bell Telephone stock.

Some sources believe Drawbaugh first dreamed of transmitting the human voice through wire as early as 1860. It was thought that he never fully appreciated the value of the telephone, seeing it instead as more of a novelty or a plaything. Drawbaugh kept no detailed notes on the development of what he called "the talking machine." In an era of public opinion against corporate America, county residents regarded Drawbaugh as a victim of big business and fast-talking lawyers. There was even speculation that covert agents of Bell had stolen design schematics from the workshop. Attorneys for Bell made the tinkerer look like a fool on the witness stand after Drawbaugh could not explain to the court why he failed to apply for a patent. On March 21, 1888, the *Daily Evening Sentinel* in Carlisle had this to say on the Supreme Court ruling:

> *The decision...in the great telephone case is a great disappointment to the people in this vicinity who had confidently hoped...the claims...of Daniel Drawbaugh...to top priority of invention would be sustained in the court of last resort.*
>
> *The old man is disappointed, but after an interview with the Harrisburg lawyer expressed the hope that a re-argument could be secured before the United States Supreme Court with good prospect of a favorable decision.*
>
> *Although the court, by a majority of one, decided in favor of the Bell patent, Drawbaugh takes great comfort from the fact that the three judges took the ground that his telephone invention had priority of that of Bell and that the entire court brushed aside the claims of all the other defendants.*

Drawbaugh was not the only inventor named in the lawsuit brought by the American Bell Telephone Company. Thomas Edison was also mentioned as someone who either invented or used an early prototype of the telephone before Bell's 1876 patent. "There were so many attorneys on the case and the interests were so diversified that the real question was not presented as fully as it would have been under more favorable circumstances," Drawbaugh's attorney told reporters. "There were six defendants and the time allowed for argument was divided between them and our case suffered by reason of this scattering. A re-argument would result in bringing out the strong points of the Drawbaugh claim." Litigation of this case dragged on for years and cost an estimated $1 million in the 1880s or about $25 million in today's money.

Drawbaugh spent most of his days tinkering in his workshop. This frustrated and embarrassed his wife, Elcetta, who thought the Wizard should spend more time in practical pursuits like farming and millwork to support their eleven children. Over the years, Drawbaugh made furniture, painted portraits of neighbors and worked such odd jobs as gunsmith, piano tuner and mechanic, but none of this side work brought in enough money, and the family was in debt to practically everyone in the village. As someone who wanted to climb the social ladder, Elcetta frequently nagged Daniel that their home was too small and not as nice as their neighbors. He took refuge in his workshop. Her overbearing personality may have saved his life.

On May 4, 1903, Elcetta woke up after hearing strange noises in the bedroom to find a man holding a pillow over her husband's head. The

This circa 1875 photograph shows the interior of Daniel Drawbaugh's workshop with his telephone device on the workbench. *Courtesy of CCHS.*

intruder ordered her to keep quiet or "I'll blow your brains out," a newspaper reported. Instead, Elcetta jumped out of bed and tried to rouse her husband. One version of this story has her opening the balcony door and yelling at the assailant as he made his escape. Once again, the gunman threatened to kill her, but her grandson Roy ran to the door and fired a gun at the stranger as he and his accomplices fled into the night. The family then rushed to the side of Drawbaugh where they found him unconscious. It was thought at first that the intruder had used the pillow to administer some kind of anesthetic, but when the inventor woke up, he showed no evidence of being drugged. Some of the rooms had been ransacked, but no valuables were taken. Though Drawbaugh believed the men were after papers or designs, there was speculation that murder was the real motive behind the home invasion.

Two nights later, an arsonist started a fire in the cellar of the adjacent home. Local newspapers reported how the flames consumed the stairways and part of the interior walls but died out due to a lack of oxygen. It appeared to neighbors that someone with animosity toward the inventor had set fire to the vacant structure so that the flames would spread to the Drawbaugh home. The family continued to live in Lower Allen Township until 1904, when both homes were sold and the family moved to Camp Hill.

Twice a day for the next seven years, Drawbaugh walked the distance between his home and his workshop at Eberly's Mill. Gradually, the commute became too much for the old inventor, who closed the workshop and moved his operation to Camp Hill. On November 3, 1911, Drawbaugh was hosting a group of reporters and local residents at his new workshop. The Wizard was excited to be close to perfecting his latest invention, a wireless burglar alarm. Drawbaugh suffered a stroke as his son was handing him an instrument. "He staggered and was unable to speak. In a few minutes, his entire left side became stiff," the *Evening Sentinel* reported. "After being removed to his home, he grew gradually worse until his death." Drawbaugh was buried in St. John's Cemetery near what is now the intersection of East Trindle and St. Johns Church roads in Hampden Township.

1909: Cash Most Welcome

Merkel Landis remembered that snowy Saturday in December 1909 when he was visited by three wise men who gave him the gift of innovation. It was evening when the shoe factory workers entered his office at the Carlisle Trust Company where Landis worked as treasurer. In the 1935 edition of the *Magazine of Sigma Chi*, Landis told the story of how he had originated the first Christmas savings club in the financial world:

> *They asked me if they could open an account in their joint names for the purpose of depositing cash each week…they proposed to collect from fellow workers…As a banker, I was interested in their proposition from the outset and listened attentively to the remainder of their story. Their idea was to start with one to five cents a week and increase the deposit by the same amount every week for the next fifty weeks and then distribute the funds just before Christmas. The account was opened and in the following week the Carlisle Trust Company announced to the public the opening of its Christmas Savings Club.*

In display ads published in the *Evening Sentinel*, the bank explained how the club would start the first week of January 1910 and would allow club members to gradually build a balance by making weekly deposits of any amount until the week before Christmas. The total amount deposited would then earn three percent interest before being distributed "just when a little cash is most welcome," the ad proposed.

Merkel Landis, circa 1901. *Courtesy of CCHS.*

That first time, bank employees had to write the amount of the initial deposit on the membership envelope, Landis explained. "To keep records properly, we had printed sheets of fifty coupons each. As payments were made, coupons were torn off and the member placed his coupons on his envelop." Checks were then mailed to members who completed all the payments.

What started out in Carlisle became an accepted practice among banks. "Our Christmas savings idea could not be protected by patent or copyright," Landis said. "Consequently, it became a purely commercial enterprise which swept through the entire financial world."

Thirty years after Landis explained its origin, Frank A. Mosher Jr. commented on the impact the Christmas Club idea has had on the American economy. As president of the Security Savings Systems of New Cumberland, Mosher was a guest speaker on the *Pennsylvania Story*, a history series produced by WHP-580, a talk radio station in Harrisburg.

"The last complete year we have figures for is 1965," Mosher said. "Fifteen million people in this country had a Christmas Club. They saved $1,800,000,000...You can be sure local merchants are very happy about this. They are great supporters of the plan. There was close to $9 million paid out locally this November."

That same broadcast, Mosher outlined the most common uses across the nation of Christmas Club funds in 1965. Of the savings, 38 percent went to buying gifts while another 31 percent went to savings accounts, stocks and bonds or other investments. As for the rest, 13 percent went to pay local and federal taxes; 6 percent paid year-end bills and 12 percent went to other miscellaneous uses, Mosher said.

Merkel Landis died at home from lingering illness in the early morning hours of September 28, 1960. That same day, the *Evening Sentinel* ran an obituary listing the achievements of the eighty-five-year-old Carlisle native. Landis helped to start the local chamber of commerce and community chest, serving as the first president of both organizations. He was the last surviving member of a group of business and professional men who became the governing board of the Carlisle Hospital in 1916. He also served as secretary, treasurer and trustee of the Sarah Todd Memorial Home since its founding in 1906. For many years, he was chairman of the local Red Cross chapter and a director of the Hamilton Library and Historical Association—precursor of the Cumberland County Historical Society.

Born on January 5, 1875, this son of John and Barbara Merkel Landis graduated from the local high school before earning degrees from Dickinson College in 1896 and the Dickinson School of Law in 1899. He later served on the Dickinson College Board of Trustees. Merkel Landis entered banking in 1901 with the merchant's bank, which later became the Carlisle Trust Company. He retained positions there as treasurer and president from late 1921 until his retirement in 1937.

Merkel Landis was married twice—first on October 12, 1905 to Helen Boyd and then after her death in March 1932 to Mary Kirtley Lamberton on August 12, 1933. He fathered two children—Joseph Boyd Landis and Katherine L. Hammersberg.

1920: Badge of Distinction

As a boy growing up in Newville, Arthur Shulenberger ran errands for the troopers assigned to the state police training academy. The first floor of the Big Spring Hotel was converted into office space, a gymnasium, dining facilities and a recreation room. One of his relatives worked as a chef in the kitchen. The upstairs guest rooms became sleeping quarters for recruits while trainers used the hotel's ten acres for stables, a horse corral and drill field. In existence for only three years, the academy was a badge of civic pride for Newville, and why not? It was the first of its kind in Pennsylvania and probably the entire United States.

For Shulenberger, having the academy in his hometown was an inspiration. The errand boy became a trooper himself and eventually rose to the rank of major. He would serve as head of the state police detective bureau and superintendent of the academy in Hershey, where it is located today. So many were impacted by the presence of the school that when it closed on March 1, 1923, the *Evening Sentinel* lamented the loss of what had been a source of much publicity and economic prosperity for the town of Newville.

On May 2, 1905, Governor Samuel Pennypacker signed into law legislation establishing the Pennsylvania State Police. The need for this agency could be traced back to the Great Anthracite Strike of 1902, which lasted over five months. Coal prices soared, causing such hardship across the country that President Theodore Roosevelt felt compelled to use his executive powers to halt the strike. Recognizing the need for a permanent statewide police force, lawmakers in Harrisburg followed through despite strong opposition from organized labor.

The Big Spring Hotel is pictured above in its role as the first state police training academy in the United States. *Courtesy of the Newville Historical Society.*

The first five years, training was decentralized. Each troop commander was responsible for making sure his officers learned the job through book study supplemented by occasional visits by other police officials and detectives. Gradually, it became obvious that a more standardized system of instruction was needed to prepare new troopers for fieldwork. In 1910, state police superintendent John C. Groome designated the Troop C headquarters in Pottsville a training facility for all recruits. The decision was made a decade later to formalize the training program by delegating this function to a special detail of men and by relocating it to a site dedicated exclusively to the development and implementation of a professional law enforcement curriculum.

The *Carlisle Evening Herald* announced on February 9, 1920, that Newville was selected as the site for the training academy. After reviewing its options, the state police signed a three-year lease agreement with landlord George Frey, owner of the Big Spring Hotel. That building used to stand at Big Spring Avenue and Walnut Street until it was demolished to make room for the Hershey Chocolate Company creamery, which later closed. Groome assigned Captain William Mair and Lieutenant Thomas McLaughlin the task of getting the academy on an operational footing, which included converting the old hotel.

Nearly a month later, on March 1, 1920, the *Herald* reported that twenty applicants had recently passed exams held in Harrisburg to qualify as some of the first students of the academy. Nearly all of these men were army or navy veterans with excellent military records upon discharge. The state police was a draw for World War I–era soldiers and sailors eager to put their service training to work in civilian jobs. The first class of thirty recruits was sent to Newville to begin a two-month program of instruction. McLaughlin was appointed the first superintendent of the academy.

Courses taught at Newville included criminal procedure, criminal law, crime reporting and investigation, traffic control, mob and crowd control, state geography (with a focus on the road network) and self-defense. Self-defense courses included the use of weapons, wrestling, boxing and jujitsu, while the legal courses touched on laws regarding motor vehicles, fish and game and forestry. Each recruit was assigned a horse and given instructions on cavalry drill, care of the animal and stable hygiene. In April 1920, the state police purchased seventy motorcycles with which to form a nucleus of a future highway patrol force. Volunteers were recruited from the field and sent to Newville for training on the operation and maintenance of motorcycles.

In a progress report covering the years 1920 and 1921, Police Superintendent Lynn G. Adams told Governor William Cameron Sproul that the last two years had seen a steady improvement in the quality of physical and mental training among the troopers. Adams described the

Cadets of the Pennsylvania State Police Training School practice riding on horseback. *Courtesy of CCHS.*

academy as an important facility for the preliminary instruction of recruits and the advanced instruction of those troopers seeking promotion to higher ranks. He added that turnover among recruits was high due to men enlisting out of a spirit of adventure only to leave the service after completing the regular two-year period of enlistment. Others found the discipline too strict, the work too dangerous and the pay too low compared to what they could make as municipal police chiefs or as officers in corporate security, according to Adams.

The superintendent also mentioned how the old hotel was in disrepair and was not particularly suited for use as an academy. "It is hoped at some future date that the department would be able to supply a building specially adapted for this important part of the service," Adams said. On March 1, 1923, the state police closed the academy at Newville and established a temporary school at the Pennsylvania National Guard Military Reservation at Fort Indiantown Gap. That school closed in the summer of 1923 and a state police training school was then established in Cocoa Avenue in Hershey. In 1960, the academy moved to its current location on East Hershey Park Drive. Reports vary on the reasons why the Newville facility closed. The *Evening Sentinel* reported that it was lack of funds, while the book *Pennsylvania State Police: A Century of Service* said it was due to the building being infested. By what, it did not specify.

There is reason to believe the state police academy at Newville may have been the first of its kind in the nation. Of the fifty states, only forty-five had joined the union by February 1920. Of the forty-five, only Connecticut, Idaho, Michigan, New York, Virginia and West Virginia had official uniformed state police agencies before Pennsylvania. According to online research, none of those states had established an official state police training academy before the one at Newville.

1922: Carlisle Cover-Up

There is no telling how many lives were saved by a bandage designated the "Carlisle Model." This sterile field dressing went standard issue with every American soldier and marine deployed to fight Nazi Germany, Fascist Italy and Imperial Japan. It was typically carried in a pouch on the equipment belt and was sealed in a metal tin, a plastic shell or a foil envelope depending on when it was mass-produced during World War II. Researchers designed it so that even a seriously injured serviceman could apply the linen gauze pad to himself. It had long tails to tie around an arm, a leg or the chest. Yet the Carlisle bandage was just one result of lessons learned from the First World War on the need for better training, techniques and equipment to recover the wounded from the battlefield.

The fighting in France showed that medical officers assigned to battalions and regiments could not keep up with their units because they lacked basic knowledge of army tactics. Some became lost for hours while the wounded suffered on the front line. The war also demonstrated a need to improve the evacuation of patients to the rear over restricted road networks without hindering the forward momentum of ground forces engaged in battle. There was also the challenge of keeping medical supplies as close to where they were needed as possible without impacting the flow of ammunition necessary to win the fight.

With that in mind, Army Surgeon General Merritte W. Ireland wrote a letter on April 28, 1920 asking the War Department to assign Carlisle Barracks to the medical services department for use as a field training school. On September

1, 1918, the Carlisle Indian Industrial School had ceased to exist and Carlisle Barracks became the host site for Base Hospital No. 31 established for the treatment of returning World War I veterans. Knowing that the need for the hospital was about to end, Ireland pitched the service school as a logical replacement. In the letter, he noted that the buildings on post could be easily converted into academic space and that a Carlisle man had offered the use of his property in the mountains for training exercises. Ireland also wrote that the local climate allowed for a change of seasons without extremes of heat or cold. His request was approved in mid-May, and the post became the site of the Medical Field Service School in September 1920.

The South Barracks auditorium became the main classroom while the rest of the building was remodeled into office space, the library and a records room. Thorpe Hall gymnasium served as a venue for sports events, school dances, receptions and large group instruction during inclement weather. The post headquarters building was used as a dormitory for officers and enlisted men. Though Lieutenant Colonel James Bevans was put in charge of the teaching staff, he first had to educate himself on army instruction methods before developing a curriculum that failed to impress some of the higher achieving students of that first class, which arrived on post in May 1921. Many of those students were World War I veterans.

Course work consisted of lectures, drills and field exercises organized under the Department of Enlisted Training and the Department of Military Art. Enlisted training taught students first aid and how to handle and transport patients. The expectation was for each man to learn how to complete basic tasks either alone or in cooperation with others, without becoming a casualty himself. In military art, students were trained in army tactics and the behavior of soldiers under different battlefield conditions. The goal was to teach students the best way to use medical units under each combat scenario.

Aside from using the post as a proving ground to test doctrine, the army established an equipment laboratory at Carlisle Barracks in October 1920 under the direction of Major John P. Fletcher. Its mission was to streamline the bulky equipment carried by medical service personnel and to design and test new products for possible use. These innovations included improved lighting for field hospitals, a field dental dispensary, first aid kits for arctic rescue units and a portable device to dispense hot cocoa to soldiers wounded on the front line.

Carlisle Barracks was one of the first army installations where field tests were conducted on the use of helicopters to evacuate wounded soldiers. Two

This Carlisle bandage box is in the Cumberland County Historical Society museum collection. *Courtesy of CCHS.*

of the aircraft arrived on post in 1935 for demonstrations before the Medical Department Board that included repeated takeoffs and landings. It was soon obvious that the small amount of level ground each machine needed made the helicopter ideal for transporting casualties. The main criticism was in the limited number of patients that could be carried in a single trip. This same laboratory also conducted the first field tests of cross-country motor vehicles as replacements for animal-drawn ambulance wagons. It was determined that a truck with four-wheel drive could navigate through thick mud, steep slopes and deep ditches with greater speed than the venerable army mule.

Of all the products the laboratory developed, the Carlisle bandage may be the most recognizable among military history buffs. World War I showed that the first aid packet then in use was inadequate for the demands of modern warfare and that an improved field dressing was needed for distribution to every officer and soldier deployed in harm's way. This new bandage had to be sterile and easy to use. Design work began in 1922 of what would later become "First-Aid Packet U.S. Government Carlisle Model." The Great Depression combined with budget restrictions limited production of the early version. An improved model was introduced in 1940, just in time for the expansion of the army prior to U.S. involvement in World War II.

Procurement of the Carlisle bandage was difficult at first. The army needed at least eight million first aid packets for its initial stock of equipment and as replacements for packets lost or used at home or overseas. Packets were first mass-produced as pressed rectangular containers that were then sealed to keep the bandage sterile. However, the brass sheeting used to manufacture the containers was in short supply, so copper was substituted in production contracts negotiated after March 1941. When copper became scarce, steel was substituted, but that changed in early 1943 when the War Production Board decided not to allocate any more steel for first aid packets.

This prompted the laboratory at Carlisle Barracks to work with the Tennessee Eastman Corporation to develop and put into production a plastic container. However, under field conditions, packets made from that material warped and broke open. Eventually, the laboratory developed new packaging where the bandage was sealed in a lead foil bag and enclosed in a waterproof box made of waxed cardboard. Not only was this cheaper to manufacture, but field tests at Carlisle Barracks proved the new material was even better than the original brass containers. The new packaging was put into production after 1943. Two years earlier, sulfanilamide was introduced to prevent infection. Soon a packet of this medication was included with each Carlisle bandage to be sprinkled on the wound. Over thirty thousand officers and noncommissioned officers went through the Medical Field Service School at Carlisle Barracks from 1921 until it was moved to Fort Sam Houston in 1946.

1936: Steam Demon

For generations, High Street residents timed their day to the rumble of boxcars and hiss of steam escaping from locomotives. When the end came, emotions ran high along the tracks as twelve thousand people gathered to watch the Celebration Special slowly advance down the middle of the street. Dressed in pioneer garb and carrying a dainty parasol, Rosie Wade was the only spectator in clothes that paid homage to a bygone era when Carlisle residents welcomed the train, its promise of prosperity and the innovation of having the first sleeper car in the world. The date was October 16, 1936, and the railroad was about to yield to progress and the rise of the automobile.

For ninety-nine years and forty-one days, trains ran through the heart of downtown Carlisle. Yet few citizens that October day mourned the loss. Indeed, the *Evening Sentinel* reported how souvenir hunters placed hundreds of pennies on the tracks to be flattened by the last train to depart town. With engineer T.C. McCullough at the throttle, it stopped first at College Street for a prearranged escort of Carlisle Borough and Pennsylvania Railroad officials accompanied by the high school marching band. Much of the crowd packed the two blocks between West and Hanover Streets with the greatest concentration in front of the passenger station that used to stand at the northwest corner of High and Pitt Streets. It was there where the engine stopped and the ceremony began with borough solicitor John D. Faller serving as emcee.

"In the name of the borough, draw the spike," Faller declared as he looked at Burgess Raymond Heckman who stood nearby surrounded by

This photograph from October 16, 1936, shows the crowd waiting for the last train on West High Street. The train station is on the right. *Courtesy of CCHS.*

workers ready at the signal to lift out the track. Within minutes, Heckman had used a crowbar to remove three spikes, and the first thirty-foot section of rail was hoisted out of the ground. Almost immediately, Dickinson College students grabbed the length of steel and dragged it down West High Street toward the campus. "Other souvenir hunters quickly grabbed up every bit of loose steel," the *Sentinel* reported. Amid the frenzy, Faller announced the official end of rail traffic on High Street.

At that point, more chaos ensued as 1,500 ticket holders tried to board the last train all at once. "There was a great crush as these fortunate persons moved forward and…others backed away," the *Sentinel* reported. "Mothers and children were separated. Smaller youngsters cried out in fear. The impatient men got testy and flared up at the milling but a…holiday spirit grabbed most." The newspaper mentioned that Heckman scolded a college freshman he caught trying to carve his initials into the side of the locomotive. Not long after, the train disappeared around a curve, and the

This photograph shows the removal of the first spike from the train tracks on West High Street on October 16, 1936. *Courtesy of CCHS.*

real work began. The station doors were locked, barred and bolted. The crowds melted away. A steam shovel was moved into position to complete the job of removing one of the last vestiges of the frontier age from Carlisle.

The town was very different in April 1835 when state lawmakers granted a charter to a group of investors looking to build a railroad from the Susquehanna River to Chambersburg. Their goal was to connect the rich farmland and iron ore banks of the Cumberland Valley to a recently completed network of canals and railways that provided Pennsylvania with a bulk transportation system that stretched across the state. Investors from Philadelphia supported the Cumberland Valley Railroad (CVRR) as a means to divert wheat grown in the valley away from Baltimore, their chief rival. State Senator Charles B. Penrose of Carlisle played a leading role in getting the charter approved. The town was much smaller back then, with about four thousand residents. The streets were dirt, the sidewalks paved with flagstones. Ox carts were common, as were pumps along the curb to provide a ready source of drinking water.

On May 14, 1835, CVRR supporters launched a stock sales campaign with backing from prominent local residents and the following advertisement published in the *American Volunteer*:

> *Today an opportunity will be presented to the citizens of this fair borough of making the...town of Carlisle...as brisk and thriving as it is beautiful. Surrounded as we are by a rich fertile country, all that is now wanted to transform our place from a*[n]*...inactive village to a splendid business city is safe, expeditious and cheap communication with Philadelphia. In the course of two years, and in all probability...one year, a communication between Harrisburg and Philadelphia will be completed by which passengers can be conveyed in the space of seven hours from one place to the other...We can leave Carlisle at nine o'clock in the morning and reach Philadelphia at six o'clock in the evening. A farmer can put his produce into a railroad car in the morning and in the same evening have it on Broad Street, Philadelphia and that too at one half of the expense it would have cost him to have it taken by wagons.*

By June 2, 1835, the campaign sold about 4,200 shares of stock valued at $210,000 or about $4.6 million in today's money. Philadelphia stockholders purchased 60 percent of the shares, while backers from the Carlisle area purchased 14 percent. That same month, supporters formed a twelve-member board of managers that directed President Thomas McCulloh to hire a chief engineer to design and build the CVRR. William Milnor Roberts was selected for the job and went about his first task of conducting a feasibility study of the proposed line. At twenty-five years old, Roberts was just hitting his professional stride as the engineer responsible for not only the CVRR but also the Harrisburg-Lancaster Railroad and the Harrisburg Waterworks. Roberts briefed the board on the results of the study in October 1835.

Roberts estimated that forty-nine miles of track would need to be laid over slightly hilly terrain to connect the West Shore of the Susquehanna River to Chambersburg. The total cost came out to an estimated $642,000 and included a bridge over the river along with the construction of buildings and the acquisition of cars and locomotives to service the line. Based on his calculations, the railroad would generate about $254,000 in earnings each year by hauling freight and providing travelers with a western link between the East Coast and the Ohio River. In today's money, these estimates translate into $5.5 million in annual revenue from about $14 million in capital outlay. The board gave Roberts authorization to proceed, and by the fall of 1836, construction was underway involving a workforce of 850 men scattered over fifty miles and supervised from horseback and carriage by Roberts and his management team.

From the start, Roberts had to contend with groups using their influence to dictate the location of the tracks contrary to his professional opinion. While one group in Carlisle lobbied heavily to have the railroad run down the middle of Main Street (present-day High Street), another group favored placing the route a few blocks to the north. This dispute was only settled after the Main Street faction won big in a local election where the railroad was a hot campaign issue. Meanwhile, Newville-area residents were upset that their town was excluded as a stop on the CVRR charter while Carlisle and Shippensburg were included. Town leaders decided that if Newville could not be on the line, they would build their own branch, and state lawmakers granted them a charter for the Newville Branch Railroad in March 1836.

When Assistant Engineer John Harper recommended that Newville be included as a stop, Roberts overrode the survey findings, prompting Newville residents to appoint a committee tasked with appealing the case before the board of managers. Roberts opposed the committee because an extension to Newville would increase both the distance and cost of the railroad. Instead, Roberts advocated a route crossing the Big Spring Creek. The board agreed to provide an extension south of town. When town residents decided to pledge $3,500 to the railroad, Roberts got angry with the managers and vowed that when the railroad was completed, he would have a pillar erected with the inscription: "This is not my line." Through maneuvering, Newville achieved the important goal of many nineteenth-century communities—a railroad link to the outside world and the promise of an improved standard of living.

The first section of the railroad was completed on August 12, 1837, and went from Bridgeport (present-day Lemoyne) to Carlisle. Dubbed the "Cumberland Valley," the first locomotive arrived in Harrisburg by canal from the William Norris Works in Philadelphia. Crews unloaded the engine at Second and Vine Streets and then placed it on a large six-horse road wagon for transport over the Harrisburg Bridge to the railhead. There, workers placed the locomotive on the tracks and made final preparations for its first journey to Carlisle the evening of August 16. Three days later, on August 19, 1837, rail traffic came to High Street amid great excitement. The people celebrated knowing that the railroad offered a brighter future for small towns.

The *Carlisle Herald and Expositor* newspaper declared the grand opening "a glorious day" for county residents. The Cumberland Valley pulled out of the

This 1991 watercolor by Eva M. Williams shows the Cumberland Valley Railroad station in Mechanicsburg. *Courtesy of CCHS.*

depot at 8:00 a.m. towing three brightly colored coaches filled to capacity both inside and on the roof with the first passengers. With the cheers of well-wishers, they left Carlisle for the West Shore, arriving at the river in fifty-seven minutes. There, the train took on passengers from Harrisburg for the return trip to Carlisle that took about forty-seven minutes. "The road was firm and true…the Engine Powerful," the *Herald* reported. The trip was repeated a few more times that opening day with "not the slightest accident…to mar the gratification of the occasion," according to the newspaper.

A special dinner was held at 2:30 p.m. where Judge John Reed proposed a toast honoring the railroad as a "common source of advantage to all our interests." Nine other formal toasts were offered honoring, among other things, the support of stockholders, the expertise of engineer Roberts and the perseverance of the board of managers. A financial panic in early 1837 had put an end to the first railroad boom in America. In his book *History of the Cumberland Valley Railroad*, Paul Westhaeffer explained how the fiscal pressures combined with a weak currency and tight credit threatened to derail the hard work of the managers who were determined to forge ahead and complete the line.

At its peak, the CVRR employed about 1,800 people and served as the principal freight and passenger carrier through the valley until 1919 when it was absorbed by the larger Pennsylvania Railroad. But within those first few days and months, county residents were swept up by the novelty of rail travel. On August 21, 1837, train rides were reserved for ladies only, prompting this report from the *Carlisle Herald*: "Such a gathering of the fair sex we never did see. We really thought the world was turned upside down and for the life of us we could not tell where they all sprang from. However, they all appeared delighted with their ride and, although the sparks flew thick and fast…We have no doubt…the ladies in thinking of the sparks thought what a delightful time it was for them to throw sparks at the gentlemen."

Almost three months later, on November 16, the CVRR opened a thirty-three-mile segment of line from Carlisle southwest to Chambersburg. Newville celebrated the arrival of the first train with the firing of a cannon while one thousand spectators had gathered in Shippensburg to watch the event as a band played "Hail Columbia." A dinner was held at a Chambersburg hotel attended by such notables as Thaddeus Stevens, who stood on the center of a table and "poured a torrent of eloquence that drowned the air with applause," according to Westhaeffer. A writer for the *Carlisle Republican* took to extremes the tendency of journalists back then to blend news and commentary when he described the reaction of the local population to the arrival of the CVRR and its first run to Chambersburg:

> *We heard that dogs dropped their tails and ran like frightened fiends, howling and trembling to the far-off mountains. Men there were too, who cleared fences and ditches at a single bound as the hissing engine approached. Others rolled on the ground and clicked their heels to express…the new delight, intoxicating and bewildering, that rushed like mighty waters upon their souls. Old men and women…gazed in visible awe as though doomsday was at hand or chaos come again while blooming maidens capered and danced and looked with more delight upon the grim besooted countenance of the steam demon than they ever did upon clean washed lovers dressed in Sunday clothes.*

CVRR started a regularly scheduled passenger service in February 1838. Back then, travelers from Pittsburgh and the west took the stagecoach to

Chambersburg, arriving there at about midnight. They then boarded the 1:00 a.m. train to Harrisburg where they connected with the morning train to Philadelphia. One day, supervising manager Philip Berlin was riding the eastbound train to the big city to place an order for a new passenger coach. Along the way, he talked with a weary traveler who had just spent thirty-six hours on a stagecoach. That person suggested that Berlin provide a railroad car with sleeping facilities. This request was the inspiration for the Chambersburg—probably the first sleeper car put into service anywhere in the world. Westhaeffer included a detailed description in his book.

The Chambersburg had a center aisle that ran the length of the car with partitions that divided the chestnut interior into four compartments. The first compartment contained several pairs of reversible transverse seats. The second and third compartments were sleeping quarters for men and were

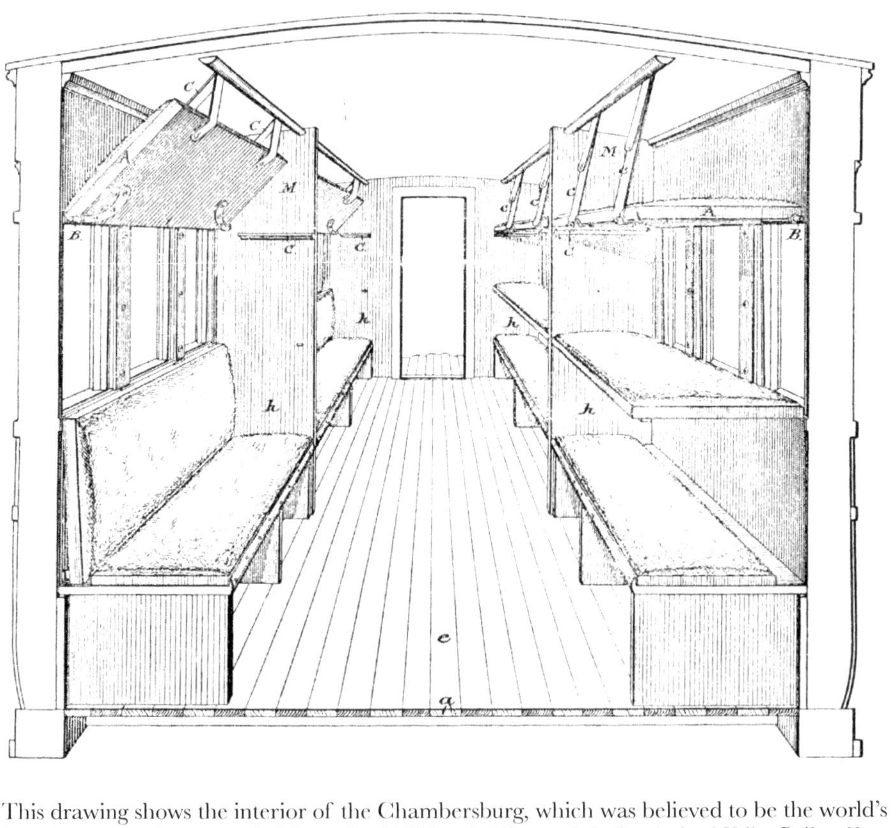

This drawing shows the interior of the Chambersburg, which was believed to be the world's first sleeper car. It was copied from the 1979 book *History of the Cumberland Valley Railroad* by Paul Westhaeffer. *Courtesy of CCHS.*

each fitted with six bunks—three along each side of the car. The lower bunk was stationary and served as a seat cushion during the day. The middle bunk was hinged to the wall and hung down during the day to form the seat back. The upper bunk was hinged to the wall and swung up during the day for storage at a forty-five degree angle with the wall. The railroad used the space behind the upper bunks to stow the bedspreads and pillows it issued to passengers using the sleeper car. The fourth compartment was reserved for women and was separated from the rest by a door with a lock. It only had a set of lower bunks along with a water closet in one corner.

There was no extra charge for the sleeper car service, and the priority on bunks went to eastbound travelers. Heat came from an iron stove located in the middle of the car. Light was provided by candles. Two conductors took turns keeping watch over the passengers and enforcing company rules against smoking, tobacco chewing and making noise. The Chambersburg was so successful that within two years, the number of stagecoach passengers using the sleeper car service doubled, and CVRR had to convert an ordinary passenger coach into a second sleeper car named the Carlisle. Both cars served as day coaches on the return trip from Philadelphia to Chambersburg.

Despite the popularity of sleeper car service, CVRR was struggling financially. In 1839, company president Thomas McCulloh spoke these words of cautious optimism: "We are an energetic and elastic people, and with care and economy, our wanted prosperity will soon be obtained." McCulloh resigned as president in April 1840. He was replaced a year later by Frederick Watts, a Carlisle attorney and gentleman farmer who later became the "Father of Penn State." In his thirty-two years as president, Watts turned the nearly bankrupt CVRR into one of the most stable and prosperous companies in American railroading history. Westhaeffer attributed this to the ability of Watts to "pinch the company's dollars until the eagle shrieked in agony."

In the decades that followed, the Pullman Company tried to protect its monopoly of the American sleeper car industry by suing companies for alleged infringements of its patents. Defendants often sought out the testimony of CVRR officials and employees to prove that sleeper cars were in common use long before Pullman invented his version. As for CVRR, it went through a period of expansion and acquisition through the mid- to late-nineteenth century. By 1889, it had reached the Potomac River and beyond to the Shenandoah Valley. It also had lines to such Pennsylvania towns as Dillsburg, Waynesboro and Mercersburg. In 1859, the Pennsylvania Railroad purchased controlling stock in the CVRR but kept control at arm's length until 1919 when it merged the CVRR into its system. By that time, railroads were starting to give way to trucks and automobiles. PRR ended passenger service in 1961 about thirty-five years after the tracks were removed from High Street in Carlisle.

Bibliography

1733: Bloody Deed

Bates, Samuel P. *History of Cumberland and Adams Counties, PA.* Chicago, IL: Warner, Beers & Co., 1886. Reprinted Evansville, IN: Unigraphic, Inc., 1975. Sponsored by the Cumberland County Historical Society and the Adams County Historical Society.

Cress, Joseph. *Murder & Mayhem in Cumberland County.* Charleston, SC: The History Press, 2010.

———. *Remembering Carlisle: Tales from the Cumberland Valley.* Charleston, SC: The History Press, 2009.

Douglas, Harry. "Shippensburg Is a Unique Part of History." *News-Chronicle*, October 17, 1991.

Fague, John. "The Shippensburg Story Part I: In the Beginning." *News-Chronicle*, March 5, 2004.

Kendall, Reverend D. Homer. "History of the Messiah Evangelical United Brethren Church, 1866–1966, Shippensburg, Pennsylvania." Information contributed for use in USGenWeb archives by Roxanne Eckenrode.

Wing, Conway Reverend. *History of Cumberland County.* Philadelphia, PA: Herald Printing, 1879.

1777: Equal to Expectations

Hoch, Paul D. *Carlisle History and Lore: Its People, Places and Stories.* Carlisle, PA: Cumberland County Historical Society, 2003.

Humrich, Christian B. "Washingtonburg." An uncompleted paper read before the Hamilton Library Association in Carlisle on February 19, 1907. Introduction by Professor Charles Himes.

Tousey, Thomas G. *Military History of Carlisle and Carlisle Barracks.* Richmond, VA: Dietz Press, 1939.

Trussell, John B.B. "Washingtonburg: Revolutionary War Arsenal at Carlisle." *Cumberland County History*, Winter 1992.

1787: A Dangerous Instrument

Cress, Joseph. "Bill of Rights Mostly Written by County Man." *Sentinel*, February 27, 2000.

Crist, Robert. *Robert Whitehill and the Struggle for Civil Rights.* Lemoyne, PA: Lemoyne Trust Co., 1958.

Hilton, John. "Founding Father Dodged Creditors in End." *Sentinel,* February 27, 2000.

McMaster, John Bach, and Frederick Stone, eds. *Pennsylvania and the Federal Constitution, 1787–1788.* Indianapolis, IN: Liberty Fund, Inc., 2011.

The Pennsylvania Historical and Museum Commission. "Robert Whitehill." www.explorePAhistory.com.

1789: This Untimely Fate

"Historical Female Pirates." www.katyberry.com/dorianne/pirate.html.

"Life, Last Words and Dying Confession of Rachel Wall: who, with William Smith and William Dunogan, were executed at Boston, on Thursday, October 8, 1789, for highway robbery." Transcript of Boston printed broadside found at www.eaww.uconn.edu/writings/wall_confession.html

Linn, Mark Benjamin. "Rachel Schmidt Wall." www.findagrave.com.

Vallar, Cindy. "Women and the Jolly Roger." www.cindyvallar.com/womenpirates.html.

1833: TRAMPS ABROAD

Dall, William Healey. *Spencer Fullerton Baird: A Biography*. Philadelphia and London: J.B. Lippincott Company, 1915.

Herber, Elmer C. "Spencer F. Baird: A World Famous Naturalist from Cumberland County." Dickinson College, 1956. Research paper.

———. "Spencer Fullerton Baird and the Purchase of Alaska." American Philosophical Society, 1954. Research paper.

Long, Barbara Phillips. "Dickinson Professor Gives America Its Attic." *Sentinel*, February 27, 2000.

Stuart, Douglas Baird. Excerpts from a speech made at the dedication of the statue of his grand-uncle Spencer Fullerton Baird.

1838: MOBOCRACY

American Volunteer. "The Crisis." December 20, 1838.

———. "Historical: Cumberland County's Part in the Buckshot War." A five-part series that published on January 15 and 22, 1882, and February 1, 8 and 15, 1882.

———. "Major General Samuel Alexander." December 20, 1838.

———. "Outrage Upon Outrage." December 27, 1838.

———. "Senatorial Conference." January 3, 1839.

———. "Senatorial Election." January 21, 1839.

———. "The Soldier's Return." December 27, 1838.

———. "Sublimation of Meanness." January 3, 1839.

———. "Voice of Old Cumberland." December 20, 1838.

Carlisle Herald and Expositor. "Another Incident." December 11, 1838.

———. "Mr. Editor." December 27, 1838.

———. "The Crisis." December 14, 1838.

———. "The General Order." December 27, 1838.

———. "The Military." December 27, 1838.

Cooper, John M. *The Buckshot War.* Chambersburg, PA: Kittochtinny Historical Society, 1903.

Snyder, Charles. *The Jacksonian Heritage: Pennsylvania Politics 1833–1848.* Harrisburg, PA: Pennsylvania Historical and Museum Commission, 1958.

Stellino, Tracy. "Ritner Establishes State's Public Schools." *Sentinel*, February 27, 2000.

Wing, Reverend Conway. *History of Cumberland County*. Philadelphia, PA: Herald Printing Co., 1879.

1840: This Lovely Earth

Bates, Samuel P., and Jacob Fraise Richard. *History of Franklin County, Pennsylvania.* Chicago, IL: Warner, Beers & Co., 1887. Reprinted Evansville, IN: Unigraphic, Inc., 1975. Sponsored by the Greencastle-Antrim Civil War Roundtable, Greencastle, PA.

The Beacon. "McCormick Homestead to Trust." Published by the Pennsylvania Conservationists, Inc., July 1983. Organization newsletter.

Blymire, David. "Carlisle Boasted 'Father of Penn State.'" *Sentinel*, February 27, 2000.

Clouse, Jerry, and Kate Kauffman. "Watt's Folly." *Pennsylvania Heritage*, Fall 1989.

Fletcher, Stevenson Whitcomb. *Pennsylvania Agriculture and County Life 1640–1840.* Harrisburg, PA: Pennsylvania Historical and Museum Commission, 1950.

Murphy, Jan. "Rock Provides Tribute." *Sentinel*, July 16, 1988.

Podvia, Mark W. "The Honorable Frederick Watts: Carlisle's Agricultural Reformer." *Penn State Environmental Law Review*, Spring 2009.

1847: That Oppressive Lawsuit

American Democrat. "Cumberland County Slave Case." November 4, 1852.

American Volunteer. "Important Decision by the Supreme Court." June 28, 1849.

———. "Slave Case." October 31, 1850.

Bobb, Mary. "Underground Railroad." Lamberton and Hamilton Library Association prize essay. Carlisle, PA, 1913.

Court Records of Mary Oliver et al vs. Daniel Kaufman, November Court of 1847, Cumberland County. Transcription of testimony.

Cress, Joseph. *Remembering Carlisle: Tales from the Cumberland Valley.* Charleston, SC: The History Press, 2009.

Friedman, S. Morgan, creator and maintainer. "The Inflation Calculator." www.westegg.com/inflation/.

Houpt, Lindsay. "Fugitive Slave Cases in Cumberland County, PA." *Cumberland County History*, 2010.

Lear, Joyce Louise. "The Underground Railroad." Hamilton Library Association prize essay, 1956.

Pennsylvania Freeman. "A Hard Case." December 22, 1853.

The Pennsylvania Historical and Museum Commission. "Daniel Kaufman." www.explorePAhistory.com.

Philadelphia Press. "Daniel Kaufman." October 15, 1899.

Records of the District Courts of the United States, United States Circuit Court for the Eastern District of Pennsylvania, Oliver, et al vs. Stephen Weakley et. al, Case 14, October 1849.

Tritt, Richard L. "Kaufman's Station at the Village of Boiling Springs." *Cumberland County History,* Summer 2007.

"The Underground Railroad." In *Two Hundred Years in Cumberland County*, Carlisle, PA: Hamilton Library and Historical Association, 1951.

Wing, Reverend Conway. *History of Cumberland County.* Philadelphia, PA: Herald Printing, 1879.

1859: KIDNAPPED THE KIDNAPPER

American Volunteer. "Abduction of Negroes." June 23, 1859.

———. "Court Proceedings." November 24, 1859.

Carlisle American. "Daring Abduction of Negroes." June 15, 1859.

———. "Further of the Kidnappers." June 29, 1859.

———. "The Kidnappers." June 22, 1859.

———. "Testimony in the Trial for Kidnapping." November 16, 1859.

Carlisle Herald. "Trial for Kidnapping." April 10, 1850.

Houpt, Lindsay. "Fugitive Slave Cases in Cumberland County, Pa." *Cumberland County History*, 2010.

Thompson, D.W. *Carlisle Outlaw: The Life and Times of Charley Foulk, 1837–1884.* Carlisle, PA: Thompson's Bookstore, 1975.

Wing, Reverend Conway. *History of Cumberland County.* Philadelphia, PA: Herald Printing, 1879.

1861: OUTBURST OF PATRIOTISM

American Democrat. "The Harpers Ferry Garrison at Carlisle." April 24, 1861.

———. "Melancholy Accident." April 24, 1861.

American Volunteer. "Arrival of Three Fugitives from Harpers Ferry." April 25, 1861.

———. "Our Citizens Alarmed." April 25, 1861.

Carlisle Herald. "The Harpers Ferry Troops." May 3, 1861.

———. "Melancholy Accident." April 26, 1861.

———. "A Stampede." April 26, 1861.

Evening Sentinel. "Mt. Holly's Centennial." July 1, 1916.

———. "Rebels Raided Holly Paper Mills." July 8, 1913.

Tousey, Thomas G. *Military History of Carlisle and Carlisle Barracks.* Richmond, VA: Dietz Press, 1939.

Wing, Reverend Conway. *History of Cumberland County.* Philadelphia, PA: Herald Printing, 1879.

1863: EXCLUSIVELY GENTLEMEN

Cress, Joseph. "Why Did Lee Chose Cumberland Valley?" *Sentinel*, March 7, 2004.

Evening Sentinel. "Tablet Unveiled at Spot Where Rebels Turned." October 16, 1929.

———. "Visits Sterretts Gap Fort He Held." September 19, 1927.

Nye, Wilbur Sturtevant. *Here Comes the Rebels.* Dayton, OH: Morningside Bookshop, 1988.

1863: SABER BLADE DAZZLE

"Case of William E. Miller Application of Award for Medal of Honor," submitted by General David M. Gregg of Reading, PA, June 7, 1897.

Evening Sentinel. "Capt. Wm. E. Miller Died This Morning." December 10, 1919.

Holbrook, Thomas. "Men of Action: The Unsung Heroes of East Cavalry Field." Gettysburg Seminar Papers, www.nps.gov.

Hummel, Merrill F. "Captain Miller's Medal of Honor." Essay from 1963.

Public Ledger. "Capt. Miller Dies, Disobeyed Orders, Saved Gettysburg." December 10, 1919.

Talley, Carol. "War Hero Deliberately Disobeyed Orders." *Sentinel*, February 27, 2000.

1888: COURT OF LAST RESORT

Daily Evening Sentinel. "Drawbaugh's Defeat." March 21, 1888.

Evening Sentinel. "Camp Hill Man Possesses Piece of Antique Machinery." September 21, 1912.

———. "David Drawbaugh Inventor: The Story of His Achievements." November 4, 1911.

Friedman, S. Morgan, creator and maintainer. "The Inflation Calculator." www.westegg.com/inflation/.

Lynch, Frank. "Court Hung Up on Local Phone Whiz 98 Years Ago." *Sunday Patriot-News,* March 30, 1986.

Miller, Diane R. "Drawbaugh Arson Damage Uncovered." *Guide,* April 30, 1986.

New York Times. "Court Cases." September 30, 1886.

———. "Daniel F. Drawbaugh Dead." November 4, 1911.

Reynolds, Patrick M. *Pennsylvania Firsts: The Famous, Infamous and Quirky of the Keystone State.* Pittsburgh, PA: Camino Books, Inc., 1999.

Shippensburg News. "The Great Cumberland County Clock." February 23, 1878.

Star and Enterprise. "Tried To Murder Old Inventor." May 13, 1903.

United States Circuit Court Southern District of New York, American Telephone Company and others vs. Pennsylvania Telephone Company, defendant's testimony. Harrisburg, PA: Edwin K. Meyers printer, 1886.

1909: Cash Most Welcome

"Christmas in Pennsylvania." Transcript from *The Pennsylvania Story*, a series by WHP 580 talk radio in Harrisburg.

Encyclopedia Dickinsonia. "Merkel Landis." chronicles.dickinson.edu.

Evening Sentinel. "Merkel Landis Dies at 85 Years." September 28, 1960.

Landis, Merkel. "How I Originated the First Christmas Savings Club." Published in *The Dickinson Alumnus* in December 1935. Reprinted from the *Magazine of Sigma Chi.*

1920: Badge of Distinction

Carlisle Evening Herald. "Newville Selected as Site for Police School." February 9, 1920.

———. "Twenty New State Police Will Train at Newville." March 1, 1920.

Conti, Lieutenant Colonel Philip M. *The Pennsylvania State Police: A History of Service to the Commonwealth 1905 to the Present.* Harrisburg, PA: Stackpole Books, 1977.

Derrick, Judy. "Sixty-Five Years of Pennsylvania State Police: They Came a Long Way." *Valley Times-Star*, Spring 1970.

Evening Sentinel. "Newville Gets State Police School." February 5, 1920.
———. "Police School Opens March 1." February 19, 1920.
———. "State Police School at Newville Closes." March 1, 1923.
Infantino, Marc S., ed. *Pennsylvania State Police: A Century of Service 1905 to 2005.* Boston, MA: Houghton Mifflin Company.
Pennsylvania State Police. "Pennsylvania State Police History," under "About Us." www.psp.state.pa.us.
Valley Times-Star. "Newville Recognized for Role Played in Early Pa. State Police Training." spring 1970.

1922: Carlisle Cover-Up

Kurash, John. "Medical Field Service School." www.army.mil.
Olive-Drab.com. "WWII Carlisle Dressing." olive-drab.com/od_medical_kits_ww2_ifak_carlisle.php.
Tousey, Thomas G. *Military History of Carlisle and Carlisle Barracks.* Richmond, VA: Dietz Press, 1939.
WW2 U.S. Medical Research Center. "History and Development of the Carlisle Bandage." www.med-dept.com/carlisle.php.

1936: Steam Demon

Bates, Samuel P., and Jacob Fraise Richard. *History of Franklin County, Pennsylvania.* Chicago, IL: Warner, Beers & Co., 1887. Reprinted Evansville, IN: Unigraphic, Inc., 1975. Sponsored by the Greencastle-Antrim Civil War Roundtable, Greencastle, PA.
Clouse, Jerry, and Kate Kauffman. "Watt's Folly." *Pennsylvania Heritage*, Fall 1989.
"A Common Source of Advantage." In *Two Hundred Years in Cumberland County.* Carlisle, PA: Hamilton Library and Historical Association, 1951. Reprinted from the *Carlisle Herald and Expositor*, August 22, 1837.
"Conductor McCartney." In *Two Hundred Years in Cumberland County*. Carlisle, PA: Hamilton Library and Historical Association, 1951. Reprinted from "Rhythm on the Rails" from C.H. Leeds's *Old Home Week Letters.*
Evening Sentinel. "Thousands Witness Last Train Ceremony." October 17, 1936.
Friedman, S. Morgan, creator and maintainer. "The Inflation Calculator." www.westegg.com/inflation/.

"A Glorious Day." In *Two Hundred Years in Cumberland County*. Carlisle, PA: Hamilton Library and Historical Association, 1951. Reprinted from the *Carlisle Herald and Expositor*, August 22, 1837.

Hoch, Paul D. *Carlisle History and Lore: It's People, Places and Stories.* Carlisle, PA: Cumberland County Historical Society, 2003.

Podvia, Mark W. "The Honorable Frederick Watts: Carlisle's Agricultural Reformer." *Penn State Environmental Law Review*, Spring 2009.

"Sleeping Cars on the CVRR." In *Two Hundred Years in Cumberland County*, Carlisle, PA: Hamilton Library and Historical Association, 1951. Reprinted from the *Carlisle Herald*, April 23, 1876.

Westhaeffer, Paul J. *History of the Cumberland Valley Railroad , 1835-1919.* Washington, D.C.: National Railway Historical Society, 1979.

About the Author

Courtesy of the Sentinel.

Award-winning journalist Joseph David Cress has worked as a full-time newspaper reporter since October 1990. Since November 1998, he has been a staff writer with the *Sentinel* in Carlisle, Pennsylvania. *Hidden History of Cumberland County* is his fifth book with The History Press. Prior works include *Remembering Carlisle: Tales from the Cumberland Valley*, *Murder & Mayhem in Cumberland County*, *Murder & Mayhem in York County* and *Wicked Carlisle: The Dark Side of the Cumberland Valley*.

A native of Lebanon, Pennsylvania, Cress earned his journalism degree from Shippensburg University. Aside from being a journalist and author, Cress is a novice poet, an avid music lover, a World War II history buff and a member of Starfleet International. Cress lives just outside York, Pennsylvania, with his wife, Stacey, dogs Patches and Rosco and cats Boone and Jinx.